GRI

GREEN

A Caithness Childhood

VALERIE CARR

TUCKWELL PRESS

First published in Great Britain in 2002 by
Tuckwell Press
The Mill House
Phantassie
East Linton
East Lothian EH40 3DG
Scotland

ISBN 1 86232 104 3

British Library Cataloguing in Publication Data
A catalogue record for this book is available
on request from the British Library

Typeset by Antony Gray
Printed and bound by
The Cromwell Press, Trowbridge, Wiltshire

To my family

Contents

Foreword

Whatever did children do before computers, television, videos, pizzas, crisps, hamburgers and personal stereos? How did people survive without central heating, telephones, kitchen appliances, worktops, supermarkets, and ready-prepared boxed meals? What did folk do all day in that bitter, bleak, windswept, northernmost county of mainland Scotland? Did families exist merely to defy Nature?

I was born in a small village in Caithness called Latheronwheel in 1953. Before I was five, my parents moved to Thurso, one of the main county towns. But at weekends and in the summer holidays, my sister Margaret, Mam and I stayed with my Nana and my cousin Derek at the Lodge in Latheronwheel. The Lodge was a small fusty cottage which belonged to the absentee landlord who owned the Big House and probably the village and most of the surrounding land. But the adventures we had there, imagined and real, belonged wholly to us!

My thanks to :

Alistair Lawrie
James Porter
Elizabeth Garrett

1

Pets around the Lodge

All my jumbled recollections of childhood have as their starting point – pets. It wasn't that my sister and I bought many, or were given many. Indeed, Mam and Dad kept reminding us that our flat in the centre of Thurso was no place for animals: too small a garden for rabbits; cats would be run over, dogs would need constant attention etc. etc. – adult dilemmas. But at weekends, in Latheronwheel, we amassed hundreds of animals and insects who became reluctant pets!

In my early childhood, my actions weren't led by a love of animals, more that I had an obsession to own them. Those were not the days of quietly observing nature in situ, marvelling and leaving quietly and smugly with that secret shared. No, those were the shrieking days of chasing butterflies, and collecting in jam jars as many iridescent green beetles from sorrel as I could. In fact, more than my sister, Margaret, was always best! These captive pets were soon released and the ecology of Latheronwheel recovered.

However, the pet newts were perhaps a mistake and their apparent rarity in the countryside now, something I regret and feel guilty about. Margaret and I had found the newts, quite by chance, in a shallow pool up at Knockinnon Quarry, about half a mile from the Lodge. It was an insignificant, muddy pool and really not one anyone would linger at, expecting to uncover anything as unusual and beautiful as twenty to thirty male and female palmate newts.

Burning in and out the brown silt, they flashed their orange bellies and spotted backs at us. At once, we wanted to touch their colour in our hands and behold their lustre free from clay and

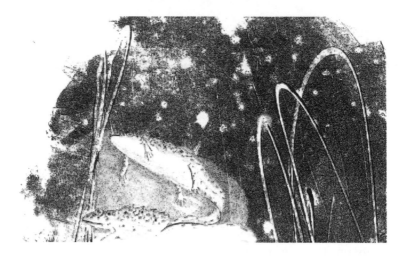

dirt. Their webbed feet and smooth skin made them miniature wonders and we wanted them for ourselves. We wanted, not just a few, but all of them. We tore home in case anyone else discovered and snatched them in our absence. We raided the dump of old tins and bottles which lay, partially hidden under a green icing of moss and lichen, under a twisted net of elderberry trees, in a hollow down from the Lodge. There we found the perfect containers – two old, rusty, paint tins with carrying handles! We sped back to the quarry pool.

Our fingers fished out the newts more gently and skilfully than a net. Our aim was to capture all of them but not hurt any. We carried them slopping back to the Lodge and carefully poured them into an old zinc washing bath. However, four had been damaged in the excitement of the trapping and we placed them in a shallow 'hospital' tank and paid them little attention. We were enthralled by the sheer number of the rest. Imagine us finding such a special catch! In the middle of all this, Nana called us in for lunch. And boy, we needed it – it had been a good morning's work and we were starving!

Washed, settled at the table and Grace said, we heard the seagulls squawking on the roof. 'Sounds like them maas are fair pleased wi' themsels. Sounds like their bellies are fill,' someone said. Realisation is sometimes slow but when it hits, it's like a brick. We dashed outside but the newts were gone. From the roof, the seagulls grinned and cackled with laughter. Mind you, they'd left the four in the 'hospital' tank. We just tipped them out. They were no good – they weren't the best. Besides we felt stupid. It would be too tiring to return them to the quarry. The game was over and we had lunch to finish.

For a long time we hated seagulls and threw stones at any within aim. That was until we chanced upon one in a field. It had been a damp weekend with a ghostly haar which hung on our shoulders like a heavy woollen blanket, making walking un-pleasant and boring with a sticky, soggy monotony. Verdant grass, lightened to a soft green with moisture, was like a plush velvet carpet; and spiders' webs hung around like stretched, silver-spangled hairnets, beaded with dewdrops. Had we been further away, the seagull would have remained completely hidden in the greyness but instead he foolishly panicked and

bounded comically and pitifully away from us with one wing awkwardly outstretched and useless. Margaret and I looked at each other and decided telepathically, there and then, that he might as well be our pet!

We caught him easily enough in our headsquares and once back at the Lodge transferred him to an empty shopping bag. Luckily it was Sunday and Dad would be taking us back to Thurso, a distance of some twenty miles, by car. (Our adventures in Latheronwheel were confined to weekends and school holidays.) Margaret and I sat in the back seat with the seagull in a covered basket between Margaret's feet. I giggled and whispered and drew attention to myself. I was hopeless with secrets. But the secret wasn't just mine, it was Margaret's too. Her determination to keep it showed resolutely and poker-faced to my side glances. It would be more than my life was worth to betray that secret to Mam and Dad. As for that bird, why he remained so silent on that half-hour trip back to Thurso, I'll never know. I suspected that he knew we'd saved him from certain death from foxes or crows, or perhaps it was utter fright, or even 'gullish' excitement. I was certainly excited – not many bairns could boast of having a seagull for a pet!

We hid him in a wooden tea-box in the downstairs shed and placed a piece of heavy-duty wire-netting on top. How long he remained hidden, I'm unsure, but he enjoyed a few swims in our bath while Mam was out shopping! He was however ungrateful and untameable: he would lunge at us with his trouser-press beak so quickly that we couldn't anticipate his actions.

Mam was suspicious of our constant offering to bring coal up from the shed – our helpfulness being exclusive to this chore – helping with other housework was as lukewarm as usual; and even more suspicious when she finally traced the stale fishy smell in the bedroom to a half-empty tin of cat food, which lay under Margaret's bed. What else would you feed a pet seagull with? After many pertinent questions and swearing and me uttering the very thing I was supposed to keep secret – 'Please don't look in the shed' – we followed Mam as she tossed me a dark look and strode downstairs to the back garden.

Amongst all the pleading that he wasn't well enough to be released, that he was sick and injured, she pushed off the wire-netting and out he jumped. He waddled along the pavement, as you would expect a poor gull with a damaged wing to do, then, to our dismay and astonishment, flapped his wings with gathering speed and took off almost vertically, and certainly raucously, and with not so much as a backward glance, flew off and lived happily ever after, I decided glibly.

For this was not meant to be a life-long friendship between child and beast. This was no bird who would follow us as an appreciative shadow, a life-long buddy who was glad to be safe and, therefore, forever indebted to us. That was the basis of a Walt Disney story and this was merely a seabird who lived by his wits and not our imaginative 'what ifs', and we weren't the famous heroines we supposed we should be. 'Whatever next?' asked Mam.

Well, there was a sheep. Margaret and I drove a sick ewe back from a field near the Lodge, one weekend. We were cautiously optimistic of our healing prowess after the seagull incident. We kept the ewe in a narrow recess between the Lodge and an outhouse and secured the gap with an old metal gate. However, it couldn't keep quiet and we were found out almost immediately. Nana and Mam shooed it back to the field amid mutterings of rustling and suchlike. Frankly, I wasn't disappointed. The animal seemed stupid and untrainable despite its dodderiness.

The Lodge was pulled down some time ago. Nothing remains, only rubble. As if to emphasise its erasure, a high wall was built across what was once the front door. How could a cottage have stood in such a small area? Yet it did and was home to Nana and my cousin, Derek, who is my age, and home to four more at weekends: Mam, Margaret, me and sometimes Dad.

The Lodge was a good half-mile walk from the village of

Latheronwheel and overlooked by no neighbours. It was, in fact, the Lodge of Latheronwheel House, known to all as 'the Big House', and the summer residence of the Palmers – of 'Huntly and Palmers' biscuits. The main drive to the Big House was tree-lined, fluorescently yellow-lined with daffodils in the spring, and was to the left of the Lodge. The Lodge was on the main road, directly in front of the Big House but separated from it by a two-acre field and not overlooked by it because of the trees. A narrow strip of garden, walled on the road side and walled on the field side, connected the Lodge to the main drive. Near the Lodge the garden was lawned and cultivated, with a clothes line strung between a tree and a pole, but at the end nearest the drive, it was wild with brambles, 'sticky willies', nettles and spiders' webs.

We had trampled down the chest-high grass to make a path to the drive. On damp mornings, gobs of cuckoo-spit encircling tiny, frail-green leafhoppers stuck around the grass and weeds like a heavy cold. The first person swiping down the path transferred these to his/her socks or trousers and also cleared the yards of near-invisible web-mesh which broke disconcertingly at nose height and probably transferred their occupants to heads and shoulders!

How fascinating spiders' webs were! Did spiders swing on web-trapezes in the night? Some of the billowing, slack tight-ropes were secured to verticals some five feet away. Tucked away in a corner, under leaves, or indeed straight across the main path and unsheltered from the elements, were sticky, wheel-spoked traps. Like clear elastic they moved with the breeze. On dewy mornings, they were illuminated with moisture and were suddenly everywhere like fairy village lights. Some were as big as towns, surrounded by communities of varying size. These dewy mornings gave us a vision which was microscopic, much like on a frosty morning when each white-edged, white-veined leaf stood proud of its neighbour and became singularly important, and the whole of yesterday's flat green lawn was now a busy, painstakingly-detailed, white pen drawing. It made us glance sideways, stop and observe instead of screeching past, as usual, with a forward vision and only a dim notion of the presence of spiders, still and silent, waiting for a catch.

I knew all about catching spiders. Nana had once told me to remove one, which was on the pantry wall, in a teaspoon and carry it outside. The indent in the spoon would fit it exactly, I had decided. I placed the spoon in front of it – it merely had to step in to be transported sedan-like outside but, to my horror, it ran up the handle and up my sleeve. Despite my yelling and arm-waving, it defied gravity, as insects can, and would not shake off. I can admire their craft, speed and agility and the way they fearlessly stalk towards people, but I do not like them.

I remember the time when Margaret and I were jumping through the long grass, on that side of the Lodge, with sticks between our legs, on horseback, and I noticed a huge spider, attached like a clasp at the back of her waist-length hair. I disliked spiders, but she hated them. I suppose I could have quietly knocked it off, but I had never seen such a giant and the effect when I told her was brilliant! As if struck by a burning

torch, her 'horse' bolted, as Margaret shrieked like a banshee back home. By the time I cantered up to her, helpless with laughter, she was stamping around snorting, 'Is it off? Is it off?' But it had long since gone and I wondered if I'd maybe dreamt it. We didn't play down that side of the Lodge much after that.

The Lodge itself was small. Up the steep stairs, which were gloss painted with a narrow strip of carpet running down the middle and held in place by brass stair-rods, were two attic bedrooms with tiny skylights. Below was the guest bedroom which smelt fusty as if dead autumn leaves had been swept under the bed, or crammed in the dressing-table drawers, or were hanging mustily in the wardrobe. But the room was clean and tidy and the grate was made ready with newspapers and kindling, in case of visitors. Under the stairs was a dark cubby-hole where Nana kept straw baskets of dusters, polish and brushes on a nail behind the door. Further back, the cupboard was too dark to probe.

On the other side of the stairs was the living-room with a small pantry at the back. This contained just a freestanding cupboard, an electric cooker (with a single oven, two rings at the back and a long flat plate at the front), and a sink. Cold water gushed in any amount at the turn of a tap, when once it had been brought home by the bucketful from a well. Hot water was a precious commodity. A basinful could be heated up for washing clothes or dirty dishes, but it wasn't then tipped down the sink and wasted – it could be used for washing the kitchen floor, or the fireplace, or the doorstep and outside path. Often it lay, cooling to grey in the basin, bubbles fading to grease, waiting for someone to think of a use for it.

The chemical toilet was, of course, outside in an outhouse. Going outside on a moonless winter's night was an experience. With the door open, darkness would press down on me and if I looked hard enough, I could see the boughs of trees moving their heavy limbs towards me. Between the wind swishing through the long grass and the mice snuffling around in the partition wall, there was no time to get comfortable – speed was of the essence!

Back inside, the living-room fire was always aglow, warm and comforting, wafting smells from soup-pan or stew-pan simmering by its side. On cold nights, we huddled round it, sitting on the brown fender boxes – our faces and fronts scorched, while our backs remained frozen. Or else we huddled round the wartime wireless set and listened to 'The Clitheroe Kid', or 'Family Favourites'. (It would not be until later that us northerners would receive a television transmission and with that, the luxury of a black and white television set.) Best of all was when we rolled back the mats and danced to the Scottish dance-music programmes. The steps we didn't know, we made up. There was a certain echo that enhanced dancing on the flagstone-covered floor, encouraging eager amateurs! Sometimes Nana allowed us to wrap dusters round our feet and we skated across the flower-patterned linoleum, avoiding the cracks, and polished it at the same time! Thus we fanned the heat round the living-room to the sound of jigs and reels and dashing white sergeants.

Suitably warmed up, we would retire to bed with a freshly baked pancake or scone and jam, and a hot mug of tea. Opening the door and stepping into the lobby on such a night, we found the coolness refreshing but on other nights, simply raw. Our bedroom was painted with icy blue distemper, a powdery emulsion, which rubbed off on our hands and clothes if we leant against it. On winter nights, its blueness made the room feel colder and sometimes we wore our duffel coats in bed and once our hats! There we would read magazines about Australia and other exotic places where it was always warm. 'Imagine that,' Margaret once said. 'In winter, folk in Australia are sweating, almost naked, on a beach somewhere.' We gulped some more tea for warmth and my chilblained feet gingerly searched between the flannelette sheets for the stone hot-water bottle, which was newly filled and red-hot.

We'd cut out pictures of kangaroos and koalas and sellotaped them to the wall and our minds would separately wander off on other adventures as the wind howled and whipped past our skylight window, cracking underneath the slates. All night the decrepit trees, which surrounded the Lodge, would bend alarmingly and we'd hear the creaking of arthritic joints as they moved inside shrivelled bark. If any had fallen, they would surely have gone through the roof and killed us as we slept. On such a night I often went to sleep with a prayer still lingering on my breath, promising to be a missionary in Africa, anything, to be spared until morning.

And the morning would be sun-filled, with the blackbird already awake and singing his sweet melody on the roof. He, too, was glad to be alive! We would rise to a crackling fire and Nana humming hymns. Once the sticks stopped sparking and the coal burned strongly and calmly, we held each item of clothing up to it, in turn, and shivered until the clouds of dampness faded, before putting each cosy one on. Then it was up to the table for a bowl of porridge, milk and sugar followed by another day of adventures.

On the other side of the Lodge, away from the drive to the Big House, was another area of thick grass up to our shoulders and dotted with more ancient leaning trees, stubbled with lichen. These were the infirm old men that I had seen from the outside toilet. Mam and Nana set fire to the grass amongst them, to keep the grass from spreading like a thick green moss right up to, and maybe, over the Lodge! If the grass was dry, and therefore crisp, the fire bolted rapidly, which left us children just watching, with our feet in tufts of warm charcoal. Far better when it was damper. Then it spread slowly and we could jump through the tongues of acid-green smoke, pausing only to close our eyes long enough to blink the nip out of them.

The smell was acrid. But we danced on and on as though we were part of some ancient ritual. The mucky smoke puffed around us and for a spluttering instant we were its centre, its flame! What fun! Half-heartedly Mam shouted, 'Give it up. You'll be reekin'.' Because she knew that from our first jump, the smoke had gone completely through our clothes, through to our skin. We might as well be naked. Like Nana before her, she'd done exactly the same at our age, and beyond the frown, she smiled. And we laughed and choked equally, until the entire patch was burnt. Then we stamped out the embers until our black rubber boots were white with ash.

Further from the Lodge the ground dipped down towards the main road and there, among the bow trees, was the dump of bottles and tins covered in a green felt of moss. Dad once made us stilts out of two sturdy treacle tins by making two holes with a screwdriver at the top of each, on opposite sides, then lacing thick string through the holes and cutting it at waist-height. Once knotted, we stood on our tins and held the strings. Those 'stilts' rewarded with the most magnificent noise as we plodded down the tar macadam road!

Just beyond the dump was the Back Road, which was a bumpy track used as a tradesman's entrance to the Big House and also access to the Gardener's Cottage, Bremner's Farm and the

Gamekeeper's Cottage. The distance between the Lodge and the Gamekeeper's being about a half-mile. It was a direction we often headed in. The starting point was the horse chestnut tree, with its conkers ripening nicely for the autumn, then along the hawthorn-lined track towards the Big House. Here, I remember Margaret showing me and Derek how she could ride her bike. No, not in the sense you're thinking of, because she had a length of rope tied to each handlebar and as she pedalled, she held onto the slack in the middle. She really rode that bike! Until she fell off. That road was full of potholes and not fit for horse-bikes!

Towards the Big House, the track became more even and it skirted round the front of the House and met up with the main drive. Walking there at dusk, we saw drifts of silvery-white ghost moths rising off the damp grass before us, while others, more brightly coloured, danced magically in and out of the hedges. But beyond the high boundary wall, the Back Road continued on, past the Gardener's Cottage, and forked right towards Bremner's Farm. The farmhouse was set back from the road and enclosed within its own lawned garden, just like a five-year-old's drawing of a house and garden of near perfect symmetry. The byres, barns and hen-houses straddled the track and were easily explored, if the coast looked clear. Hens mumbled around, moaning to each other, but it was the cats and kittens that we were interested in. Whatever colour combination you can think of, there was a cat like it. We each had our favourite and used to sneak scraps from the pantry, in our anorak pockets, to feed our own cat. Yes, these were yet more of our pets!

Being farm cats, they were stupidly shy of being petted, so we were forced to catch them and push them into a vacant hen-house. When we tired of this game of feline hide-and-seek, me, Margaret and Derek would squeeze into the hen-house with about twelve cats, of various sizes and hues, purring and being fed and stroked. This must have been the ultimate in small-space love and affection! Our only concern was running into the geese, which formed a noisy deep-throated pack of angry

Medusa-necks and trembling sticking-out tongues; or else running into the farm labourers while searching the byres.

One time, we ambushed a cat and cornered it at the bottom of a flight of stairs leading to a hayloft. It ran up the stairs and squeezed through a gap in the broken hayloft door. Now it was cornered. Like heroes we burst through the door and startled the three or four sweaty farm labourers, who were sitting on hay bales drinking tea with mucky hands. One said something and the rest sniggered. We turned round like cowards and ran down the stone steps, clipping each one, like noisy frightened stallions. Our quest to search for cats was over. We didn't play that game again.

Besides, the Back Road was very open, with no woods or trees or private places to explore, and led past the Gamekeeper's Cottage, where gun dogs were locked up in a barred pen beyond the peat stack, and barked furiously whenever anyone approached. There was no way we could pass there unseen. Therefore, the Back Road became the road home if we'd been up Smerral, of no significance and so often a drudge as we dragged weary legs home after a long day's outing. Even if we played a game of 'soldiers', by each taking a turn swiping with our plantain the tufty head of the other's, it would just be a temporary distraction. The road remains in my memory as a half-mile of agony.

2

Beyond Paradise

The other way to walk up Smerral was to follow the main road for about a quarter-mile and, once past the old blacksmith's, fork left up the Smerral road. It's a single-track road, tarred, with passing places. It was bordered on the left with wild raspberries, pink and white dog roses, and blooming daintily below them were scabious, lady's-smock, vetches and cornflowers. On the right were trees like laburnum, wild cherry, rowan and Scots Pine. In the shadow of these grew rasps and brambles, and everywhere else filled out with rushes which followed the steep line of the bank down to the burn. The variety of berries and the cover of the branches meant that this walk was loud with birdsong.

A mixture of melodies from unseen songsters, each one auditioning for some unknown opera and each one singing a different piece, straight from the heart. I've always wished that I could amble down a country lane and tell my companion which song belonged to which bird, but I couldn't then and I still can't. Despite being in the country, we only knew the names of the most common birds and identified the others by their species, i.e. 'hawks', 'finches', 'crows'. How difficult it is to spot a bird in a tree! Many a time I've stood right below the exquisite song and peered up into the branches and, just at that split second when both eyes focus on that dark shape of bird . . . it flits off and becomes invisible again.

It was a productive walk up the Smerral Road. In the summer we ate a bellyful of rasps, checking, when we remembered, for those tiny yellow maggots and discarding rasps with any inside. If we had a bag, or any container in our pockets, we would collect them to eat later in a bowl with milk and sugar. Between the heat in our pockets, the large amount of berries and our jumping and stumbling, we usually took home a puree!

Walking up the road was the easy option, but straying from the road among the trees and swishing through the rushes into the deep dips and hollows which Nature had formed was much more exciting. In springtime, we would suddenly come across bright clumps of double-headed daffodils and great mounds of snowdrops, swelling steadily annually to twelve inches or more in diameter. Untouched in their secret places, time had allowed them to multiply. But the real find was the day I explored deeper and discovered the wild orchids. They were quite the most beautiful flower I'd ever seen! I stared at the abundance of purple and mauve lying regally around me. I picked just a few of each colour, attempting to force the memory of them to last a bit longer and then tiptoed out from amongst them, like an intruder. Early each summer, I returned to prove they were no daydream, and each summer I was enchanted by them.

We always brought bunches of flowers back to Nana. We were careful to pick just a few from each clump and learned by experience which flowers were too delicate to survive the journey home. For instance, a bunch of primroses contrasted with just a few dog violets looked a pretty posy, but the violets soon went limp, and that sprightly charm they had possessed on the grassy slope, withered too. So we contrasted the delicate, pale yellow primrose flowers with their flat, broad, hairy, green leaves. This is, after all, as Nature intended – that hint of yellow was delicate only relative to the coarseness of its leaf and surrounding grasses. A handful of different species of flowers, the same colour, was one idea we tried, but the yellow of the celandine seemed brash and vulgar alongside the paleness of the primroses.

Summer turned posies into bouquets of roses, clovers, vetches, campions, ragged robins, harebells, poppies and so many others, and scents into Chanel! There were plenty of junior aspirin bottles rinsed out and waiting to be filled with perfume, in an outhouse at the Lodge. Junior aspirin was the cure-all for all ailments from headache, earache, toothache to boneache. Illness was tolerated and untreated and certainly not worth wasting the doctor's time with. He had to come from the next village and there was no sense in dragging him away from something more urgent, from someone more ill – and anyway, 'If your time had come, your time had come'. It was as simple as that. Besides, the little orange tablet tasted pleasant enough and the empty bottles were the right size and shape for perfume. The scent mixture was no secret: 85% water, 5% sugar, 8% flower petals and 2% luck. Derek remained unimpressed.

There seemed about three drawbacks to collecting wild flowers for perfume in summer. One, was that the most tiny, most intricately interesting, white flowers of goatsbeard and the umbelliferae stank; two, was that the sweetest fragrance came from the most prickly shrubs, like dog rose and whin (honey-suckle was the exception but its scent is so sweetly pervasive that a vase of it was constantly moved from room to room in an attempt to dilute the fragrance); and three, was the flies.

In spring, vertical lines of delicate-winged flies quivered in the fresh warmth of the sun. Even in early summer, they were a minor irritant. But, come July and August, they came from everywhere – dark, hard, noisy and menacing like mini, remote-controlled helicopters, attacking. We wore blue; we used bracken for swats; we tied thin chiffon headsquares over our faces as we yelled and tried to outrun them along the burn and up the Strath. We saw nothing of the marsh marigolds, nor the monkey flowers in the burn, nor did we hear the gentle lapping of water over stones as the crystal-clear stream made its way to the shore. Instead, was a monotonous din of flies. Margaret, being older and with longer legs, found that if she overtook me, her flies would join the growing, angry, bulbous mass around my head.

Mam said flies liked me because I was sweet, but that was no consolation now. Still, it was possible to run quite far up the Strath, past the hazelnut trees, on and up the burn to more open country. Thankfully, the majority of flies tired of flying almost as

soon as we tired of running and we could, at last, pause, and take down the gauze-layer of headsquare and feel the sun on our faces again.

But the chase had been real enough. We had hurtled along, translucently looking ahead with veiled eyes, as if in a blinkered dream. Scarf-restricted vision had snatched at passing outlines and gathered fuzzy pieces of them for my brain to analyse and make sense of. Meantime, hearing became the more important sense and was left to interpret the buzzing and imagine it as anything it wanted – and it made much of this opportunity. So the noise became a menace which chased and bullied and touched. Although I still ran, my feet were unsure of the path and faltered in mounds and hollows. The 'menace' was tripping me up. Soon it would pass me and grab me and stop me and I'd have to scream and I'd have to look at it – all unsightly and horrible. My legs were tiring, my chest thumped and all across my brow, beads of sweat were competing to run down my nose.

I had to stop and wipe my face. It was time to open the headsquare, that morning curtain, and count to ten and leave that dreamt-up monster unremembered or, hopefully, dissolving in the daylight. As I lowered the chiffon headsquare to face the unfaceable, the brilliance of the sun shone on my face with an intensity which made me blink. Behold! We stood in a wondrous place of green vegetation, flowers, birdsong and the sun dominant in a rich-blue, cloudless sky. Was it still a dream, or had we stepped into paradise?

Perhaps we'd hurtled back in time to the very beginning of existence, pre-man and pre-dinosaur. Time had stood still there, where dragonflies still ruled the insect world, long before wasps and ants. Here, they flew confidently, fearlessly and stick-like along the narrowed burn.

We could now inspect the marshy tufts for frogs and linger on a small flagstone bridge and dangle our legs over the side, allowing them to find their own rhythm. We were the only humans here. With childhood immodesty, I felt Eve-like in this paradise of warmth, scent, and abundance of flora and fauna through which trickled the burn, like a pulse of life. We ate our Ayton Sandwich biscuits and rejoiced with the lark.

Unsatisfied and unhumbled in paradise, inquisitiveness made us search beyond – just to look over the next boundary, round the next corner, just to see something more and maybe better. Humans, unlike dragonflies, cannot remain for millions of years in the same spot, even if it is the most perfect habitat. We always feel there could be something better, somewhere else, and so begins a journey of discontent, a pursuit of happiness with no reward. So, being human, we ventured onwards. We found ourselves in a boggy area where wild mint grew like a crop. The smell was soporific. It permeated all our sinuses and was deeply heady. I feared we might stumble drunkenly into another dream, and where would we find ourselves then? Not paradise, to be sure. Those legs took over again from a drugged brain and searched for dry tufts to use as stepping stones out of the marsh, just to go on a bit further.

Beyond here, the open hill was stark and rough. Sweet-smelling whin flowers were borne on spiky branches. Rabbits darted uneasily in every direction and kestrels hovered overhead. Peewits called in high-pitched squeals, anxiously and without rhythm.

We lay back on a bank and felt the energy being sucked out of our legs and replaced with a chilling worry: we'd only walked halfway, we still had to get home. But sheer exhaustion can be euphoric and we easily closed our eyes, hoping for the sun to re-energise our boneless legs, to get us home.

Time did not limit our adventures, for we had no watches and no way of knowing how long we'd been away, it was Hunger which brought us home. And if wishes were dreams which could really be granted, I wished that day for a magic carpet to transport our tired bodies home.

With half-open eyes, and then half-open mouth, I saw a slow,

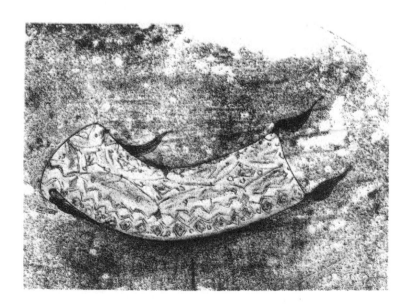

elegant, flat, grey shape float by. Was this another trick of the dream-state? Another adventure I'd be forced to act out? Would the carpet indeed take us home, or somewhere else, or another time? Would it fly so fast that our limp bodies would merely tip off? Would I enjoy it? Would I be scared of being high up in the clouds? Magic carpets usually responded to instructions, though. 'Look! A heron,' shouted Margaret. It was indeed a rare sight, but I had wished for something rarer.

It was the call of the curlew which touched a raw nerve inside us and its wincing sharpness made us edgy and exposed and lonely. It alerted us and warned us that we'd strayed too far from home. Now the adrenalin flowed into our veins and we took to our heels and ran recklessly home on concrete legs. Our flight home was as speedy as we could manage. I might limp a section with a stitch in my side, but Margaret was hungry too, and not sympathetic. 'Come on, or we'll never get home!'

It seemed but a few short weeks that we could walk around in short sleeves and actually wish for a slight breeze to cool us. The rest of the year, being exposed to the wind was something that we just got used to – Caithness is mostly treeless, except for a patchwork of pine plantations through its centre. Unprotected coastal villages are slapped by north and east sea gales. The shelter of the Strath was, then, like a rich oasis of vegetation and wildlife. Summer came and the sun, like a snake charmer, teased flowers, shrubs and weeds from their drab, worn-out winter beds to meander skywards and open out resplendent. Around this fragrant palette of colours danced dark tortoiseshell and red admiral butterflies, bumble bees and also, hidden underleaf, clegs or horseflies.

It amazes me that a skin, sensitive to the first probing steps of a minute spider or tiny greenfly, cannot feel such a large fly land and greedily suck blood from bare skin. Then, not satisfied, they maliciously inject poison into the wound and cause that limb, or suchlike, to harden, swell and itch and itch. They are pernicious insects. An evil in paradise.

3

Of Mice and Men

Our trips out usually had to be purposeful. We never returned home empty-handed, for instance. We could bring back a bunch of flowers, sticks, herbs, berries, a swede, insects or other reluctant pets. It seemed natural, like some primitive 'gathering' instinct. Usually this was confined to Latheronwheel.

However, I once visited a road safety exhibition in Thurso Town Hall. There were large glass display cases, the bases of which were painted out with roads and pavements. Along these pavements ran about twenty, well-schooled, white mice, who only crossed the roads at the zebra crossings. Young onlookers knew that the mice got a mild electric shock if they jaywalked. But the sight of all those mice herding together, just like the newts, was fascinating.

So we learned, like the mice, that we should only cross roads at zebra crossings. But Thurso had none then, and none for another thirty years! So what else were we to learn? That the High Street was electrically charged, perhaps? I would make sure that I wasn't in the first bunch of kids to cross the street outside the Town Hall – just in case! Visions of children taking giant leaps, trying to cross it in eight strides instead of ten, and arriving at the other side with instant, tight perms, made me chuckle!

What then, had been the point to it all? Tall, uniformed policemen stood around straight-backed in surly bunches talking to each other, while little children weaved noisily in and out of them and the display cabinets, mimicking the mice. If they had intended us to learn something, the message was enigmatic and secret. Perhaps they preferred to keep it to themselves and whisper it to each other? Perhaps the message was that they could at least catch white mice? Or, perhaps they wanted us to think that they could catch us, just as easily, and keep crowds of us confined in glass cases? Perhaps I had been looking for a point, when there had been none?

But I had spent all day there, reflecting on it, wasting so much time, that I felt compelled to ask a policeman for a mouse, to take home. There was nothing else for it! From two feet above my head, his rigidness intact, he muttered something I didn't quite hear. I stood there, puzzling over the possibilities of what he could have said. When I looked round, I saw him take three strides towards a case, fish around in the tails and withdraw a white dangling thing. 'There.' And he plonked it headfirst into my cupped hands. That's how I came by 'Tufty'.

Unfortunately, Mam couldn't share that sorrow I saw in his huge pink eyes. Perhaps he wasn't a particularly bright mouse, and who knew how many electric shocks he'd accumulated that day? Reluctantly, Mam gave him the safe run of the seagull's vacated tea box. Safe only for a few months. One day, Mam spotted a cat scarpering from the open shed, the lid of wire netting on the ground, and no Tufty. I prefer to think that Tufty actually escaped before the cat was seen, found a mate, had a family and taught them, in the first instance, to avoid crossing roads, and hopefully, to avoid cats.

Tufty, before his 'disappearance', soon became an effort to look after. Once the initial delight of putting him up my sleeve a few times and watching him bulge about in my clothes, tickling as he explored, and once the greater delight of surreptitiously placing him on an adult's shoulder and awaiting the scream, had both been experienced – there wasn't much else a mouse, for all his cuteness, could be expected to do. So cleaning him out and feeding him became a chore. Always, as I picked up my pyjamas, Mam would remind me about Tufty. Tutting too loudly was inevitably followed by, 'You wanted it . . . you brought it here . . .' Off I'd go, torch in hand, to the shed. There was something quite

stomach-turning about feeling the soft lumpiness of a slug under slippered feet. Why so many slugs slithered into the shed at night I never knew, but it put me off slugs and mice.

But Tufty had one redeeming feature: he became a handy excuse for not going to the Salvation Army on a Wednesday night. The excuse being that I had to clean him out, of course. He was incredibly stinky for his size. I loved the Salvation Army and still hold it in high regard. It was the 'Mercy Seat' that I couldn't come to terms with.

After attending regularly, my friend Carinda told me that it was my turn to approach the 'Mercy Seat' and silently confess my sins to God. Two things bothered me: one, was feeling vulnerable out there in front of everyone whispering behind my back; and two, was not having any sins to confess. It seemed sinful to make some up. Did the amount of time I might sit there for matter? Say I sat for five seconds, did that prove I was 'good', or merely 'dishonest'? Conversely, if I sat for too long, counting up to something like twenty, did that show I was 'bad', or just a slow counter? There were too many 'what ifs' . It was easier and safer, conscience-wise, to clean out Tufty.

But the other Wednesday nights that I went to the Army Hall were great. I loved the familiarity; the gaiety; the tambourines with the colourful ribbons flowing to the simple beats; the songs with the compelling choruses, the fun; the enthusiasm oozing that God loved children and we loved Him too! I couldn't believe that God could change so much by Sunday.

In Latheron, after walking over a mile to church, dressed in our Sunday best, complete with compulsory hat (how I prayed for my head to outgrow my red felt hat with its two white, furry pom-poms dangling down the back, which tied under my chin with too-tight elastic), we would sit quietly in the cool dim church with the rest of the congregation, on hard wooden pews, listening to the dourest of organ music. Eventually, the melody got louder and the bars shorter and more triumphant, as the dark-cloaked minister took his place in the pulpit, above us.

Now we were scolded for being sinners. There was no laughter here. The minister launched into a toneless diatribe, as all of us hung our heads in remorse, or ignorance. When he talked of evil people, did he mean all of us? Was he looking at someone in particular? Should we all turn round and stare at someone evil? But no, his judgement was over all of us, and generally, he didn't rate us highly. I sucked harder at my pandrop sweetie.

It was a relief when the sermon was over and we could step out into the brightness, and the holy silence that was the Sabbath. For Sundays were quiet days. Days to reflect and be hushed and respectful and Christian, not loud and vulgar and childish. The sun around the church was frail and limping and old in years. Adultness hung around like a bad smell.

The minister, the tall dark man of God, stood at the door of his church and shook each hand in turn, nodded and smiled. I always hoped his handshake would be spectacular and would tingle in my palm with a spiritual energy which would radiate through my body, so that I would exit the dim church as a small shining bulb of eternal light, keen to do His bidding. But his handshake was firm and clammy and the only sensation I felt

was that it was over too quickly. I felt no presence of my God. He must have rushed overhead, onwards to Thurso, to the Salvation Army Hall, above which He listened and joined in the actions of 'If you're happy and you know it clap your hands'.

But meanwhile, in Latheron, castigation over, villagers chattered freely and friendly offers of lifts home by car were readily accepted. What people wore was noted and discussed in detail later by the grown-ups.

Most Sundays were just that: sunny days and, coming at that end of a sometimes dreich week, something to worship indeed! So a Sunday was an obvious choice for finishing jobs like painting or gardening, which had been postponed by a wet Saturday. But Mam and Nana were always cautious about working on Sunday. Nana had been brought up to uphold the beliefs of the Free Church, which was very strict about not working on Sundays: meals would be prepared and tables set on Saturday nights and Nana was only allowed to pin up her Saturday-plaited hair.

Enforced rest was nothing less than hardworking crofter families deserved. They worked all the hours of daylight and semi-darkness until blackness blotted out their vision. Only then did they rest by firelight or lamplight, before retiring to bed and snatching some sleep. Even with the coming of electricity, for which most were thankful, I would still come through to the shady front room of the Lodge, late of an evening, and find Mam and Nana, knitting pins clicking, thick in conversation and hunched round the light of the fire only. Dialogue dulled as the embers faded. It was possible to estimate how long they'd be staying up, by the amount of coal on the fire. If the chat needed more chewing over, an extra lump of coal would be thrown on. Once finished, they hurried to bed with the darkness, and the Lodge cooled down as we all slept till morning.

On Sundays, after we'd all been spruced up for church, Dad would come in the afternoon and we'd all go off for a run in the car. Sometimes we visited Nana's two unmarried sisters and her mother, my great-granny. She was an amazing woman who lived into her late nineties, frail in body but lucid in mind, who was often prompted into giving the family lineage of people the adults couldn't properly piece together. Without hesitation, she spoke softly and generously about folk and events deep in history, in the 'olden days'. When this adult conversation got into full swing, heavy and animated about people I didn't know, I would look around for something to distract me – a picture I'd not noticed before, anything. It was painful to have to sit for hours in my best frock, listening to the tick-tock of the waggedy-waa getting louder, while Boredom perched above me like a wicked puppeteer, pulling my strings and making my legs flop noisily this way and that. 'Sit at peace, Valerie Anne!'

Sometimes Margaret, Derek and I were allowed to escape to the garden but first we had to get past Feorag, the Cairn Terrier, which slept, ear cocked, in a box under the sideboard. It guarded the door to the scullery, our exit. It always snapped at our ankles, yapping high-pitched, coming at us like an angry ball of steel wool. It never bit us but there was always the promise of it in its deep-throated gargling. We always ran past it, just in case. More embarrassing than all of its threats was the adult laughter which also bayed at our heels.

Yet it was bliss to be outside and away from musty old tales. On a warm summer afternoon, the spicy scent of lupins was overpowering. Even Feorag was temporarily tranquillised and allowed us to stroke her. And Sunday was stitched out there in an embroidery of cottage flowers, all looking their best, never dull or faded or broken, but bright and perfect and neatly sewn. Too soon, we'd be called in for high tea.

The living room, which had sparkled with lilting conversation, now tinkled with teaspoons and glinted with best china, patterned jam pots full of home-made jam, sugar basins, butter dishes with curls of butter, side-plates, cups and saucers, all laid out on a blue-white linen tablecloth. Two tables had been pushed together in front of the fire, to form one big makeshift table. Gentry could not have dined so comfortably or so finely. Plates of bread and butter and cake stands of home-made queen cakes, pancakes, scones and slices of fruit cake, gingerbread and Madeira cake, all temptingly waiting to be tasted and approved of, were laid out at hand.

Us bairns took our places on stools with extra cushions on top. The tea was poured. Grace said. And we began. I had my eye on the biggest queen cake and a slab of fruit cake but the thick slice of tinned ham had to be tackled first and then at least one slice of bread and butter, which would be offered and could not be refused. With every bite, my slice of ham seemed to get larger. I cut bigger chunks with my huge knife but it only took longer to chew and then swallow. Someone else, someone quicker, was already stretching a hand towards my queen cake. Ah well, there was plenty on the table – a veritable feast! The home-baking was simple, always the same variety and always tasty.

I learnt at Nana's elbow how to mix a pancake batter, how to spoon it onto the hot griddle and wait for the bubbles of batter to pop, before turning them and cooking the other side. Nana made an excellent clootie dumpling: a suet-based fruit pudding wrapped in a cloth, or 'clootie', and steamed in a pan of boiling water for a few hours. Nana never weighed any of the ingredients. Instead, everything was added to the mixing bowl until it 'looked right'. Jam, likewise, was bottled when it 'sounded right'. At the time this seemed daft. But I tried it myself when I was much older and in possession of a jam thermometer and, sure enough, there is a distinctive heavy plopping sound to jam which is boiled long enough.

Jam, pancakes, a packet of tea or biscuits were always given to folk we visited. There were no telephones to make prior arrangements, so impromptu visits were the order of the day. Nana's philosophy was simple: if you brought something, you would be made more welcome. In this way, gifts were exchanged and we, in turn, took home things like scones, marmalade, carrots for soup etc. It wasn't unusual for neighbours to leave neeps and tatties on the doorstep, if they were passing and Nana had been out.

It was the custom for villagers to help with the potato picking in the autumn and, in return, each household was rewarded with a sack or half-sack of potatoes. On one occasion, Margaret, Derek and I volunteered to go up to Sam Sinclair's, at Knockinnon, to help with the tatties. Mam tried to warn me against going. I must have been quite young, or else naive, for I imagined that I just had to fill a bag of tatties and return home. Simple. I didn't realise that I was expected to put in a full day's work.

The cold day started cheerfully enough. My spirits were high with the novelty of it all. I laughed my way up the hill, as keen as the frost. Once there, the coldness nipped at my face, erased my smile and sucked at my fingertips, through my mittens. In my rubber boots, the blood at the tips of my toes tingled and began to curdle. Steadily, a cleg of coldness pulled at my skin, sipped out the blood and replaced it with a whitening weakness.

Midday came and we were all treated to a hearty meal at the long table in the farmhouse kitchen with its polished flagstone floor. The warmth, laughter and food were temporarily energising. But out in the frosty field, the tractor steadily and relentlessly turned over yet more drills and the field stretched out before me like a long nightmare.

Rubber boots had never felt so cold. My toes throbbed for the last time and grew into stone roots which stuck solid in my boots, bored through my soles and penetrated the ground, so that I could not move. The suckering cold then grew upwards through my veins until my body felt arthritic and numb. Under this wicked spell, I was bending and curling into a withering old woman. Even holding the hessian sack for others to stoop and fill, became an enormous effort. I was becoming dangerously frail. If someone bumped me, I could crack and break into pieces like an eggshell.

No-one seemed surprised when, to my own astonishment and relief, I plucked up courage and asked to go home. I was no help to them. Annie, Sam's sister, offered me a kitten to take home. I was momentarily attracted to its soft spiky fur and its large sad eyes. But I was insensitive to its vulnerability and its 'petability'. One overriding thought kept repeating in my head, 'I must get home immediately.' Rudely, I said nothing about the kitten, nothing at all.

I sped down the field, scarecrow-stiff, as if my life depended on it. My running legs moved with an automatic, disjointed motion, for although I could feel the tops of my boots flapping against my legs, whipping and burning them, lower down my feet felt wooden. Noisily, I sniffed back a tumult of tears which longed to gush down and ice my face. I sobbed them back while meaningless, high-pitched vowels bellowed from my throat instead. I didn't know myself. Back at the Lodge, I thanked God for answering prayers, for giving me a mother to hug, and for the blazing fire in the front room of the Lodge.

With joyful agony I toasted my solid blocks of feet at the fire. It was painful waiting for the blood to advance with sharp daggers into my frozen feet, scraping and clawing them back to life; but also it was blended with happiness – to be home, safe and loved! And in that instant, my ambition to be a farmer's wife was forever laid to rest.

4

Winter, Fire and the Black Rabbit

Rubber boots had never felt so cold as on that day, tattie-picking. There was a lesson to be learned, though: it was no good pulling on two pairs of thick socks, for extra warmth, and packing my feet into my boots so that my toes were squeezed against the sides – far better to look out a pair of boots that were a size bigger. That way, feet kept warmer, even if the boots were rather unmanageable.

Despite the energy-sapping cold, the countryside around Latheronwheel became an extended playground to us bairns. The idea of spending daylight hours around a lovely fire, in adult company, was a non-starter. Was it that without the luxury of central heating and without the ability, therefore, to wander from one cosy room to another in search of privacy, we felt inhibited by the one-room heating, one-room living at the Lodge? (Central heating was part of neither town nor country life then, anyway.) Everyone naturally congregated towards the fire and we were absorbed into adult conversation and adult discipline.

Instead, we needed to be children, childishly. So, we'd dress up appropriately and Mam would open the door to our outside stage, kiss each cheek in turn and shout behind us, 'DON'T BREAK YOUR LEGS!' Out we'd go to an applause of birdsong, with a sunny spotlight overhead and a stage which stretched for miles and miles in every direction. We didn't shiver nervously in the wings, instead we burst out boldly and played our part wonderfully and spontaneously! We were children and proud of it! We cared nothing of world affairs or neighbours' affairs. Our life was school and Latheronwheel and, all wrapped round us like a winter scarf, was our family.

Winters in the '50s seemed so much colder with windows iced up inside and out. Hard frost made fields twinkle with encrusted, solid, jammed-in diamonds and trees were dusted in flour like long-bearded, lank-haired, ancient wise men. Or, when it snowed, snow was stacked up against every dyke and packed into every crack by the wind. Crofters who lived in outlying districts, stocked up early with winter provisions in case they were isolated by a crisply-starched, smoothly-ironed, white linen tablecloth of thick snow, which prevented them from reaching shops and food vans from reaching them. But they didn't panic. They were used to it.

Besides, snow cleansed otherwise dank days, when fields and tracks leaked mud, and misty dampness seeped through clothes and entered the skin like a debilitating virus, bringing misery and apathy. Then, like a breath of spearmint, the air was cool, refreshing and sharp and I'd awake, feeling oddly warm, push open an unusually heavy skylight and, lo and behold, everything was pure white! Everywhere was still and hushed as a Sabbath. I

struggled to see angels smiling in the snow-ivied branches of the trees. It was so serene and heavenly that I half-expected to float through the open skylight, like Wendy in 'Peter Pan', and join the angels who were around, somewhere. But my feet were heavy and gravity a spoilsport.

Instead, Margaret, Derek and I dressed quickly, then, eyes hungry with anticipation, leapt joyfully outside. Around the Lodge the snow hugged the ground and lay moulded like wrapped-up Christmas presents. Everywhere was smooth with white fondant icing and twinkling sugar. So sweet, so tempting to jump into a smooth deep patch of white virgin snow – one where no animal or bird had yet left its mark! Only great pioneers knew this feeling. There was pride and compulsion mixed in it. Now it was time to lead the team and explore familiar haunts, disguised by snow to look unfamiliar. Behind, we left the adults with their snow-moaning, fun-spoiling expressions and their offhand gruffness: 'For goodness sake, keep the door closed. You're making the fire smoke.' To them, snow was a nuisance that they feared with a slippery, ankle-breaking uneasiness, and an inescapable slushy inevitability. They banked up the fire and awaited our wet return.

But we'd waited month after long month for this. Snow at last! We beamed up the Back Road with snow creaking like ghostly dry floorboards underfoot. Then, strangely, the snow first levelled the deep ridges in the soles of our rubber boots, then continued to grow spookily underfoot, until it increased our height by two or three inches. We teetered and tittered on these natural platform soles for a wee while, then knocked off our extra inches against a dyke.

Now it was time to try out the two plastic tennis rackets which we polar explorers had brought. We took it in turns to haphazardly lace them to our rubber boots with string. Then we could waddle across deep drifts of snow, our weight evenly distributed on these makeshift 'snow shoes'. We had seen Arctic explorers wear something similar. But the pride in our ingenuity was short-lived as one, or both, of the rackets would swivel round to the front of our boots and we'd land thigh-deep in snow. No matter what configuration of lacing we tried, believing each new one to be the perfect solution, we'd always end up slotted into a deep drift.

Tiring of this, and the sun melting the snow somewhat, to make us damper, we could now turn our attention to making snowballs, or snowmen, or great meteors of snow. All these required moist snow. All activity stopped as soon as our boots got wet inside, or our hand layers of woollen socks and mittens got sodden. When fisted fingers and curled toes then began to tingle, when faces drained to a sickly-white and eyes watered with welled-up melting ice and never with tears, and when someone suggested it was time to return to camp to check on food provisions, then we all gallantly went home. Just in time, as distant plump apricot clouds were changing to grey in a darkening sky and would soon drop their snowy swarm of crazy white flies to menace our already cold faces.

Once indoors, we rowed up our sopping-wet socks, gloves and hats in front of a wonderful fire and listened to them sizzle on the hot tiles, while we drew in our chairs and drank cups of steaming tea and ate pancakes, our cheeks rosy and aglow like glorious cherubim!

And the snowday was just as we'd always dreamt it would be, and ditto for Mam and Nana. However, their expressions were straight-lined to our curves, with a told-you-so look to them. They wished away our snow. Too soon, it ran with slush.

Now we had to walk the main road and not the sappy fields. There wasn't much me and Margaret could collect on our winter walks. Nana was 'iffy' about hawthorn but very definite that ivy, which grew on trees and on rocky shelves up the Strath, was 'unlucky'. Instead, Margaret and I brought home twigs, tree moss and feathers and glued them into shoe boxes to make miniature desolate landscapes, complete with deciduous 'trees' and 'vegetation' of moss and lichen. With a bit of patience, it was possible to make quite a complicated, satisfying scene.

Clear frosty days, when the sharp tinkle of the robin's song was matched only by the keenness of air – fresh and invigorating as a medicinal vapour rub – were days to collect sticks for the fire. Directly across the road from the Lodge was a dense wood, surrounded on all sides by drystone dykes. We called it 'the Planting'.

In spring, the Planting floor opened up suddenly with the bright-pink brushes of butterbur flowers, which were swept thickly under tall, as-yet skeleton trees. But, come summer, when the overhead tent of buds burst open and so blotted out the light, making the Planting floor dark and damp, broad leaves of butterbur started to multiply thickly and evenly, like a green hairy mould. Step into the Planting now, and our legs were invisible below the knees.

In the dimness and cooled sunlight, an active imagination could conjure up many a slithery festering monster of gigantic length, moving stealthily forward below butterbur leaves,

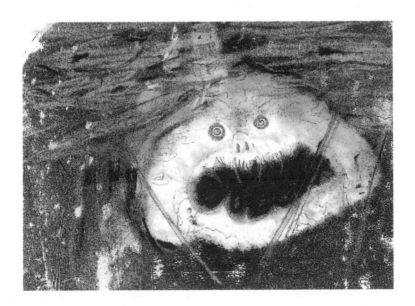

listening for movement, looking for tender legs with large eyes, nose twitching, mouth slavering, waiting, patiently waiting, to ambush tasty children!

I could have been sensible and held up each foot, to check it was still there, but Time was still and dark and slithering and chuckling and laughing and grabbing at my ankles holding me back from sun and fun and tomorrow. My legs were being sucked into the ground, bit by munching bit. The chill of the Planting ran through me and wanted me, but I kicked myself free, yelled and screamed at the silence and ran like hell past a bemused Margaret until I thankfully and breathlessly scrambled up the furthermost dyke of the Planting.

It wasn't a place to play in. No movement of earthly life was ever heard in there. At nightfall, ghostly noises rose which were caught in gnarled branches and ripped in spectral shrieks. Only an owl was comfortable in that eerie atmosphere, and even with the bedclothes pulled over my head, I could still hear its deep 'Poo, poo'. I prayed those nights that Nana had locked the front door, but, alas, that was not the country way.

The Planting was not, therefore, conducive to play and anyway it was too damp for finding dry starting sticks. Before pre-packaged firelighters, fires were built up with a base layer of tightly-screwed-up newspaper, then small kindling, and next, small lumps of coal, or else logs. A fire of dry logs soon snapped up into an inferno, which smelt wonderful, but was in danger of bolting up a too-sooty chimney and setting it alight; it made a mountain of ash in the ashpan; and it would need cleaning out daily. Emptying the ashpan into a newspaper the next morning, resulted in wide-cheeked puffs of dust wafting in clouds round the living room. Sometimes this reassembled mountain of ash would spontaneously relight itself in the newspaper, burning a hole and defeating the whole purpose of the newspaper being a wrapper. Then the burning embers of wood ash would have to be located and chucked back into the fire, and the process of getting rid of yesterday's ash would start all over again.

Once coal was teased into lighting – an art which some folk have and others don't (Mam, when she went to school in Latheron, was always put in charge of the dominie's stove, which heated the classroom in winter: he had no patience for children, or a fire, which needs a gently, gently approach) – it would glow orange and we would sit round it with slices of bread on forks, faces and hands burning like torture until the bread finally furled like dry autumn leaves. Then we'd draw back our forks in a cloud of steam, or smoke, and one side of our bread would be unevenly toasted. Then same again for the other side. But it would taste both crisp and soft and much better than toast from an electric toaster.

Some mornings, always the coldest ones, the yellow fire would flash fiercely through paper and kindling and then blackly refuse to tackle the coal. Another compilation of paper, sticks and coal would be hurriedly assembled. If this didn't 'take', then patience flew out the window and other methods were sought: skelps of lard could be smeared on chunks of coal; waxed bread-wrappers could be stuffed into cracks in the base of the pyramid; or, as a last resort, a double-page-spread of newspaper could be held carefully against the fire opening. 'Carefully', because immediately there would be a great, magnetic pull on the paper which created a huge 'suck'. Behind the paper a furnace raged and if the holder wasn't attentive and a corner dipped inwards, then the whole sheet was ablaze and had to be dealt with. This tactic, albeit dangerous but thrilling to observe, always worked.

On dim winter afternoons, we'd draw in our chairs and stare into a melting Martian landscape. We peered into the fire, as if into a crystal ball which would reveal our future. If we had an empty, paper sweetie bag, we'd point in a corner of it until it lit, then set it upside down like a hollow tent, on the edge of the grate. If it then wooshed up the chimney, we could wish a 'wishie' and it was sure to come true. What a delight to have a fire!

Sometimes we went on family expeditions to collect starting sticks and, other times, we bairns went on our own. We learned to take only old dry wood – whin was best. Then we broke it into smaller lengths, just under our knees, and carried it home in Nana's wicker basket. Any wet branches were stacked against a tree to be collected another day, once they had dried in the wind.

The best place for whins was the Shore Park. It runs alongside the Planting and we entered it by first going over the Whale Bone Gate.

The 'whale bone' was reputed to be the jawbone of a whale brought back in whaling times, when fearless fishermen roamed the northern seas. Whaling, rightly, disgusts young people now, but to poor crofter-fisherfolk of former times, a beached whale was a godsend, bringing both food and oil for lamps. It was cut up and shared around. These were times when there was no government help, no Social Security and no pensions. Folk then survived by their own effort, their own luck, or a neighbour's kindness. There was a community inter-dependency on which all relied, and in old age, when will was tethered only by weakening muscles, then old folk grudgingly allowed their

children to help them. I suppose we collected sticks for Nana for part of that reason – to repay a kindness and, besides, it was no effort to return home with a basket of sticks, after an adventure in the Shore Park.

So, we climbed over the gate, looked up at the awesome jawbone, and jumped into the Shore Park. It was an open field, full of rabbits, bunches of thistles, bunches of whins, and bunches of sheep. In the summer, newly sheared sheep with diagonal slithers of shortly cropped wool and bright-white skin, acted nervous and seemed self-conscious about being bare-naked. Others, that had missed the shearing, wandered around with their tattered fur coats, loose about their shoulders and backs, and rubbed off what they could on barbed-wire fences – as if they were scratching an annoying itch. Soon they would be dipped in the Shore Park, frantic and fearful, heads forced under the mix of chemicals, twice, with a long crook, and then separated from their chubby lambs. For days, the fields would be noisy with the shrill cries of lambs and the distant hoarse echoes of their mothers.

Going through the Shore Park by the direct route and jumping every three-foot-high thistle in sight, it was possible to reach Latheronwheel Harbour in ten to fifteen minutes. Directly parallel to our route, a wood dipped steeply down to the burn and we could clearly see the village of Latheronwheel above the trees. The village, with its whitewashed cottages all facing south for maximum warmth and end-on to the smack of sea gales, made a daisychain, edging the road to the Shore. If we chose to walk closer to the wood, then it provided maximum privacy from prying eyes in the village and also meant that we could stumble across roe deer, or rabbits, sneaking out of the wood to graze.

Here the land undulated so steeply in parts that hidden valleys were formed and we often startled rabbits who had believed these private places were secret. Much time was wasted on a thrilling, but always unproductive, chase for more reluctant pets. Every stage of rabbithood could be observed whilst running, from infant kitten to plump adult – scurrying brown/grey shapes with white flashing scuts.

In the confusion I thought I saw a black rabbit. What was it? A pure-black wild rabbit? Never! No country folk kept rabbits as pets, since rabbits were widely regarded as vermin, or at best, dinner. So this was no escaped rabbit. Where did it come from? What were its ancestors? Was it a Guardian Spirit of all rabbits? A primeval form? Or did it just evolve? I stopped in my tracks. Hesitated. Nothing – nothing but pairs of brown pricked ears above the bracken. Was it a slip of the eye – an eye usually keen and precise but sometimes coloured with invention?

'Did ye see thon black rabbit, Margaret?'

'Yes. Weird, wasn't it?'

Where did it go? It seemed to disappear into thin air. If only we could get the quickest of second looks.

The others easily leapt over the dyke, or darted into an impenetrable mass of spiky whins. The wrath of the east wind sweeps straight from the sea across that open treeless expanse of Park. Only sturdy shrubs and plants can withstand its constant beating. Whins, like spiny hedgehogs, hug the ground tightly and multiply silently each spring, to make a veritable, impassable thicket. In sheltered patches, thistles and foxgloves likewise increase, undisturbed by the sheep that sometimes graze there.

All the time, we ran on under that vast dome of northern sky in a flat landscape with no middle distance. Our vision was limited only by the peaks of Morven, the Scarabens and the Maiden Pap in the south, or by the weather. But we were forewarned by faraway dark clouds, of impending storm and the need to seek shelter. Our actions were influenced by the sky and weather, as many generations before us had been.

We also ran for fun. Running downhill was best. We could take off at speed like spinning tops – arms circling, mouths vowelling noisily, heels clicking backsides as legs gathered ferocious speed and feet found any grassy hold and we sped faster and faster downhill, out of control. We didn't care if we arrived at the bottom upright or not, but we never fell, except on purpose. However, the frenetic momentum always carried us well past our intended stopping distance. Running was joyful!

We never ran because we were late. Anyway, we didn't have watches. We knew the time approximately, not necessarily by observing the height or decline of the sun, nor by the openness of specific flowers, and certainly not by blowing a fluffy dandelion clock and relying on the number of puffs it took to blow all the seeds away. That was for toddlers who knew nothing of time – except for dinnertime and bedtime!

An appreciation of time was something from within, much like wakening for an early morning journey, just five minutes before the alarm clock rings, that sort of thing. An instinct which is not precise to the millisecond as with a digital watch, but one which is 'near-enough' or 'roundabout', and accurate enough for a child in the country to whom Time is a playmate and not a governor.

On crisp evenings, at twilight, we were drawn somehow to the 'Tulloch' – a grassy mound in the Shore Park, which was said to be a Pictish burial chamber – and lit an armful of whins with stolen matches. We watched the redness eat each branch, its jaws munching with devouring greed. The sticks cracked like aged bones and ancient spirits cackled in the warmth and rubbed cold dry hands together, then held them out like fanned peacock tails in front of the fire.

The sum of my knowledge of the Picts was one adjective, 'warlike'. I was told in class, in great detail, about southern history, of lowland Scots heroes and English kings. Yet here, I sat in an ancient land, of unknown deeds, with warlike phantoms and fed a fire.

I ran round and round the barrow with a lighted stick aloft, not knowing why, but as my torch shortened, cold sharp fingernails stroked the crest of hairs on the back of my neck. I thought I heard sniggering and snapping and brawling. The chill of history ran through me and scared me. I stopped and

rammed my fiery wooden wand into the fire and waited until it flashed through to its orange core. Then the glowing embers quickened and nervously flickered yellow. Suddenly a puff of wind gathered them into a ball and blew them away, magically, to become distant eyes of scattering light rushing back to the safety of the Tulloch. Instantly, the fire was dead. Only ash remained.

Hushed greyness became hard black and merged with the night. So we rose and ran home, safe with the knowledge that we could make fire. This primitive knowledge, so fundamental, the essence of survival. With fire came light, warmth, hot food, conviviality, family, friends, talk, love and laughter – without it, despair. So what if I was sticky on the seven times table, or I'd forgotten some of the names of Canada's Great Lakes? I could set a fire. And if, in winter, our lives depended on our intellect, then it was our self-taught, instinctive knowledge to which we referred and not what was school-taught.

The latter we would use later, when, as mini-adults, we would ponder the infinite, worry about nuclear war and nuclear waste, knuckle down to exams and wonder about careers. We would then worry with a teenage intensity – a worrying more acute than an adult's – an adult who has worried and come to terms with worry and is able to pigeonhole it. Adults have the benefit of experience and hindsight. This we would, in turn, come to appreciate but not yet, for we were still green and impulsive and exuberant and happy.

But at the back of my mind, the image of the black rabbit niggled and remained as a harbinger of doubt, of things unknown and unexplainable. A doubt that could be put in a pan over the fire, to be reheated and stirred round again and again, like the base of an adult worry: a chronic worry that can be added to and made more substantial. A worry that simmers. A worry that smells tasty and makes one hungry for more.

5

Dear and Sweet Things

Old folk should have more worries than parents. However, I don't recall Nana being consumed with worry. Instead, I remember her as a small slender woman, slightly bent at the shoulders with a glowing autumn-ripe skin, smooth as alabaster and slackened only around her eyes to accommodate a radiant summer smile – one which was warm and safe to bask under. A model might have spent much time and money to achieve such a complexion, but Nana only dabbed on any cream now and again, and sometimes olive oil in the summer.

Her once auburn hair became a glossy white with yellow threads combed through it. Parted at one side and held off her face with two kirby grips, it flowed thickly down to her shoulders, like thistledown. She sang and hummed constantly, as starlings in winter sunshine after a feed of mash – contented and casual but without their clamour. She was a woman of all seasons, of the earth itself.

She was the image of everyone's granny: softly spoken, always smiling, seldom scolding, never unkind or bearing grudges. No malice furred her arteries. She was through and through a good Christian woman. I would have called her 'Christian' even if she had never attended church, for she was self-effacing and charitable. She possessed a pure goodness which is rare and should be widely recognised. Being a child who hoped to escape her plainness and become 'famous' one day, I felt Nana should become 'famous' too, for she was a paragon of goodness.

Instead, she excelled in her ordinariness. Her house was neat and tidy but not prettily co-ordinated with matching flowery

prints: the so-called 'cottage look' which is the accompaniment
to having money and time for idle thought. She had no airs and
graces, nor aspirations towards grandeur. But she made a home
that's fire was blazing; its kettle was steaming, and tempting
smells wafted from its oven. On its window ledge, there was
always a vase with a handful of mixed garden flowers, and inside
and out, singing, she busied herself as happily as Snow White in
the dwarfs' cottage and I blushed, embarrassed that I would want
to change her, and jealously, did not want to share her either.

She was simple and wholesome and needed no added
garnish. She made a broth from rough vegetables, pulses and a
ham bone into a smooth, thick and delicious main meal, which
was even more flavoursome the next day, somehow. Then the
salt meat would be cut from the bone, divided up and eaten
with clapshot – a mashed mix of potatoes and swede with a
generous dollop of butter. A meal which lagged our bones for
many hours, keeping out the fun-stopping cold.

For she knew about bairns and fun and laughter. And she
knew about coldness and the melting joy of a flickering fire. If
we heavily returned from a tiring adventure, to a fire blackened
with dross, she easily poked it into a red rage of flames,
muttering and spluttering from heavy slumber into a fury of
warmth.

She was of another time. A time of lamplight and candlelight;
of clocks loudly ticking away the hours until fishermen returned
from the sea; of mending and knitting; of cutting peats at the hill
and collecting water from the well; of walking the cow to
common pasture; of plumping up shallow straw mattresses with
more chaff in the autumn, making them regal and splendid; of
saying Grace; of reading the Bible; of thanking God. A time
when neighbours helped neighbours carry mats and mattresses
outside for spring airing, and so winter's staleness was swept
out, communally. There were, therefore, no hidden corners, no
visible secrets. People's houses varied, not by their contents, but
by the characters of their occupants.

We children would draw our chairs round Nana and the fire, and she would talk, with specific detail and emotion, of the 'Olden Days'. Like the time she went to Glasgow, during the First World War, to work in an ammunition factory. She told of the living conditions in the boarding houses, of when the women working the next shift rose from their beds, and those who had just finished their shift got straight into them; of when some chemical dust was blown into her face, she received no medical attention, and after being blinded for a week, her sight gradually recovered but remained permanently poor. And when we edged to the brink of pity for that hard life, like a professional storyteller, she would twist the ending and we'd all laugh at some funny side to it all. For she wanted no pity. What was done, was done. And in an instant, old fusty cobwebs were laughed away.

She didn't hanker after her past life. She was a 'here and now' person. She swapped her oil lamp for an electric bulb, and her pounds, shillings and pence for 'new' money, just as a crofter accepts the heavy rain that flattens tomorrow's harvest and fishermen accept holes in their nets. What will be, will be. The unrelenting rain and bitter wind, which skimmed straight off a leaden sea, held no mysteries for her.

But as time passed, she sat longer by the fire, staring into its flickering depths, with the idle fascination of children watching drops of rain dribbling down a window, and unknowingly biting her nails. How long had she sat there? What troubled her? Quiet and deep in thought, she sat like a philosopher in repose. Just at the moment I felt I'd intruded into something private and forbidden, and should tiptoe away, she would look up and her erstwhile bland face would brighten richly into a warm smile, 'Ah, it's yersel. Time for a cup of tea?' Like someone glad that the spell of the fire was broken, she'd rise and be Nana again.

I think one's memory snaps a photograph of someone from the past, and it is this likeness, stilled in time, that it carries round in its album, to be shown to the mind's eye whenever that person is mentioned. To me, Nana always remains a sprightly septuagenarian. Indeed she had the legs of a youth! She could walk! She had speed and stamina evolved through generations of walkers, who had daily covered miles to shops, or school, or church, or hill. With scissor's strides she cut through the countryside and we infants struggled to catch up. Once along-side, she would begin, 'I mind the time when . . . ', and continue a yarn about spots on our route, spots which had never before held any significance to us, and we listened ravenously. After-wards, we remembered that place fondly, forever.

She was an interesting companion on a walk and a friend when parents scolded and hurt a green spirit. She talked in dialect with local words which teachers forbade us to write in stories, or use in verbal replies. But 'proper English' is some-times cold and unflowing and without the depth of meaning that dialect has. Words like 'cloored' (dented), 'ferfochen' (ex-hausted), 'foosim' (filthy), 'perjink' (very polite), and so the list could go through an alphabet, all of Caithness dialect words which are more rounded, with more meat on them.

Only old folk, without the aids of modern education, retain these ancient words and use them in conversation, while young people listen and more and more speak English with a Caithness accent. So, little by little, our dialect is being lost. Perhaps Nana was uneducated in a scholastic sense, but in the tides and weather; in land, sea and earth, in survival by God's infinite mercy and pre-God superstitions, she was erudite. She advised simply, 'Be happy. You're a long time dead'. A simplicity which is exact and obvious and often dismissed flippantly as such, without enough thought. For, she was not only reconciled and content with her lot, but also possessed a generosity of spirit which was freely given to benefit others. To me, she was the epitome of 'good', and by being close to her, I hoped some of her 'goodness' would rub off on me!

Of us bairns, she demanded nothing. But we thought of her constantly and happily did anything for her. Of course, if she

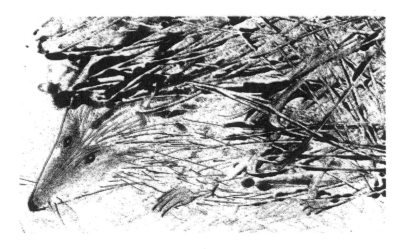

offered us thruppence for sweeties in return for going a message to the shop, then we never refused the money! Kemp's shop was in the village, just short of a mile from the Lodge. We would set off slowly along the main road, anxious for any distraction. One day, Margaret and I came across a hedgehog.

Had we found him on the return journey, then it would have been easy enough to take him home, for a closer inspection. However, we had an errand to run and the hedgehog would have to wait. After due consideration, we put him into Nana's wicker shopping basket and carefully looped the rigid handle over a tree branch, so that the basket became a swing-boat. We decided, thus confined, he would at least have fun until our return!

Capturing the hedgehog was easy, compared to choosing our sweeties. Kemp's shop, as I remember it, was a long dark store with a flagstone floor and was stocked like a smuggler's cavern. Hessian sacks of newly-polished red apples shone in the semi-darkness like rubies. Square tin boxes of individual varieties of biscuits were sold loose, by the half-pound. Milk, bread, hams, cheese, vegetables, tins, packets of this and that, were stacked from floor to ceiling. Smoking ice-cream from the dry-ice freezer was immediately wrapped in newspaper to keep it frozen and also to prevent the packet sticking to fingers, soaking up their warmth, and 'burning' them.

At the bottom of the shop, fancy things like small ornaments, aprons, lacy traycloths, wool, gloves, socks, etc., could be bought. But it was just beyond the top counter which held the best treasure – sweets! All temptingly rowed up.

Should I blow all my money on a Fry's Five Centre Bar with exotic fruit flavours? Or, how about a Five Boys' Chocolate Bar which had five boys' faces in relief, with expressions ranging from extremely happy to intensely morose? By rubbing the silver paper, it was possible to transfer their expressions from the chocolate bar to the paper, all of which made the bar last longer.

Gob Stoppers lasted longest but there was no way children could keep them in their mouths for more than two or three 'sooks', because they might miss a colour change. A Gob Stopper could start off as a bright blue ball but there were many nuances of blue, pink, and green to suck through before reaching a small hard white thing, by which time fingers were colour-streaked and sticky.

Sherbet was another sticky thing, but tongue-ticklingly fizzy. There were Sherbet Dabs – a pink lolly in a flat bag of sherbet, and Sherbet Fountains which consisted of a liquorice straw in a yellow tube of sherbet. It was difficult to suck the sherbet up the straw, so we usually ate the straw first and tipped the soggy cardboard tube into our mouths, allowing the excess sherbet to drift onto our clothes.

There were liquorice bootlaces, liquorice straps, liquorice torpedoes and liquorice pipes with pink candied beads of fire. There were candy cigarettes, and hot cinnamon Lucky Tatties, so called because there was a toy inside. Puff Candy, Highland Toffee, Penny Sweeties, and Flying Saucers (round coloured shapes of rice paper with sherbet inside), were rowed up with Fruit Spangles and Old-Fashioned Spangles. The Old-Fashioned ones had a weird taste and were strange colours. I liked the yellow-ochre ones best. There was pink Bubble Gum the size of a half-crown and, if a bairn could get two or three of them in his mouth and keep them under control, my word, he could blow a bubble to be proud of!

What would I spend my sweetie money on? Would I had enough to buy everything! But there would be more days to sample sweeties from Nellie Kemp's best counter. Even when my choice was made, I would glance at Margaret's selection and wonder if I'd change my mind? But what about the hedgehog?

We walked with some urgency back to the tree where we'd left him dangling in mid-air. But the hedgehog was gone. I looked around for the stunned, or even dead, acrobat but he had left without a trace, unhurt. It was a long time before we saw another. I bit hard on my Five Boys' Chocolate Bar, to mask my disappointment.

6

The Hedgehog, (Education) and the Fox

I remember, when in the early primaries at school in Thurso, being set an exercise listing animals into columns headed, 'Fast' and 'Slow'. I had written 'hedgehog' in the 'Slow' column and was given a tick. But that was before the Tufty days when I had to creep down to the shed on dark nights, to feed him. Mam's words would still be resonating in the living room: 'You took him here. You said you'd look after him. You . . . ' Adult advice.

Around that time, in the lamplight, I saw a small cat or large rat, scurrying at speed along the lane by our garden. I followed out of curiosity, and discovered, with disbelief, that the creature was a hedgehog! It was only then that a spark of scepticism about the truthfulness of all the facts I'd amassed at school all those years previously flickered in my brain.

Mine was an education system of straight-lined desks, tables by rote, knowledge spoon-fed, learnt and regurgitated for tests. Perhaps even if I knew, when I was seven, that I could have written 'hedgehog' in the 'Fast' column, I would still have written it in the 'Slow' column, without even daring to qualify it by scribbling 'sometimes fast' in brackets, if my teacher believed the hedgehog to be a leisurely animal.

Her authority and discipline were absolute. Unlike Mam, she entered into no discussion and no compromise. Why she bothered to learn our individual names, I'll never know. We could have been numbers instead for she treated us *en masse* – a group of ignorant souls to whom she mercilessly imparted her knowledge and view of the world. Her knowledge was not to be questioned. She was always right. Had I stood up and bravely declared, 'But I've seen a hedgehog run fast', there would have

been a hushed silence, quickly followed by laughter and mock-
ery by my fellow pupils and I would have been sent swiftly
outside for my insolence, and for the rest of the year and perhaps
more to come, I'd have been labelled a 'troublemaker'.

Knowledge was two-dimensional: facts learned, words written. 'A hedgehog rolls into a ball when approached by a dog.'
But had anyone felt the mottled prickles and noted how they
criss-crossed to make the skin impenetrable? 'Sheep "baa" but
rabbits make no sound' belied the heart-chilling, pre-death
shriek of a rabbit – a cry of fright, like a baby's scream, echoing
back to the very beginning of time. 'These wild flowers are not
found in the far north of Scotland' – yet my scrapbooks swelled
with such 'rarities'.

Delicate flowers were pressed in between pages of heavy
books, or in newspapers under mats in the passageways of the
Lodge. Many lay there, forgotten. The pressed flowers would then
be recovered the following spring, when mats were flung on the
washing-line and beaten. But they were now in a faded filigree
state – their precious beauty preserved, but brittle like thin ice.

These sneaky secrets we kept to ourselves. It seemed, the more
we looked at Nature, the more was revealed to us. This was an
education which was special and dreamlike, as silent as sunlight,
as warm as a summer breeze, and we flitted on the sounds and
smells of our knowledge like immortal fairies.

Had anyone in my class seen Fear? I saw it in the eyes of a fox
up the Strath. He was caught by one foot in a snare. The narrow
wire dug into his foot more and more as he struggled. Margaret
and I only wanted to set him free. But we were as afraid of his
unpredictable actions, as he was of ours. Fear faced Fear. Eye met
Eye in a combat of nerves. Nothing was said. Panic shuddered
through his russet body, staccato-fashion. We spoke in cloyingly
sweet voices to calm him. But his lip curled, revolted by our
human stench. He longed for death, and had his hideous
scrambling somehow snapped his arteries, he would have died
worthy of that wild thing that he was. For he was no 'gentleman

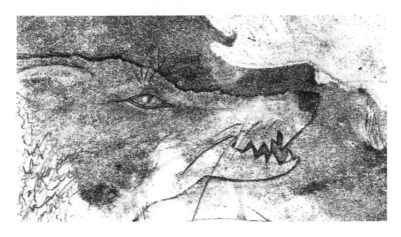

with sandy whiskers' who was 'eager to make our acquaintance'.
He was indeed handsome, but did not speak, and we were part
of no Beatrix Potter tale. How would he look in a suit and
waistcoat?

And in the seconds wasted on such absurdity, my veiled and
dreamy eyes missed how he broke loose, with the snare still
attached to his leg and rattling behind him, dislodging small
stones, as he swept downhill into the bracken, which eventually
swallowed him up.

He was free, but not free of the snare. We felt an uneasy joy. I
suppose we had effected a contradictory compromise. Did he
finally escape from the snare to lick his wound and become a
tenacious hunter again? Or, did the snare remain, always to
reveal his intentions noisily, so that he died of hunger, painfully
and without the dignity of a hunter?

We never knew the ending. Misgivings about the fox and
snare were like the dry ingredients of doubt, vague and simple,
but not yet ready to be mixed into something solid and adult and
to be brooded over. Instead, we ran screeching homewards,
hurdling every tall foxglove in sight, putting distance and
merriment between us and thoughts of the fox.

We moved as free spirits: earth children belonging to no time, or any time. This was our Garden of Eden and we ran through lushness untethered, without teachers and their doubts, their grievings, their rules, their 'real life', their 'here and now', their 'world events', their wars and uncertainties, their desire to educate us into small moulds of themselves, to stifle our freedom and confiscate our fun and put it in their bottom drawer. This weekend playtime was enjoyed in no concrete yard, restricted by walls and rules and fear. There were no boundaries here. We needed no notebook and pencil. Instead, eyes looked, fingers touched, ears heard, nose smelt – all with an acuteness much greater than enforced 'paying attention'.

In early summer, high in the vast dome of northern sky, eyes saw swifts arching and dipping, screaming their return. Lower down, swallows sped with open mouths above cornfields, hoovering up flies. Quite often, at the height of summer, when the burn rippled, relaxed and sun-sparkling down to the Shore, we would make a journey upstream, jumping from one exposed boulder to another, totally enclosed in trees, birdsong and tinkling water.

Sometimes we joined swallows travelling at breakneck speed, at knee-height, finding an abundance of flies in the shade and dampness of the burn. Our presence did not frighten them. Indeed, I admit to being scared into an infant statue on a rocky base, anxious that they would fly into me! They weaved in and out me like chaotic balsawood boomerangs. Only when they had had their fill and moved downstream into dappled sunlight, did the blood creep nervously back into my petrified legs and they could leap on, to catch up with Margaret.

Lining the burn grew 'brambles'. They are not proper brambles, but are more like a cloudberry and were introduced from Canada, I believe, and self-seeded over many years to form a thicket along the burn – and wherever else they could get a hold. I haven't seen them anywhere else but Latheronwheel. After I married, I took a seedling back to my home in

Stonehaven for my children to sample the fruit, and also to hide an old shed. I was amazed how rapidly it grew into a huge bush, sending out tens of suckers from the roots and only kept in check by constant mowing. We have since moved to another house and I often wonder if the new residents have to fight their way into the back garden!

These 'brambles', as we called them, grew to at least nine feet high and the juiciest berries were always tantalisingly just out of reach. Plump apricot-coloured berries, and surprisingly, also purple-red berries are formed on the same bush. Reaching the berries, which are easily pulled off, leaving their soft husk attached to the bush, was some sport. They have a bittersweet taste and, like 'forbidden fruit', it was tempting to over-eat. Always when I'd had my fill, I'd spy the biggest one of all. 'I'll make that one my last,' I'd tell myself, lying. Over-indulgence always led to a colicky stomach that evening!

Did the swallows over-eat at the burn? On evenings in early autumn, when the cool sun cast long shadows of wigwam stooks camped in cornfields and the wind rattled the dry peas in the pods of the broom, creating an eerie incantation, swallows dashed round stooks, zig-zag, in-out, chase-me catch-me, skirling and swishing on tireless wings like spirits bewitched.

Furtively, the 'crop spirits' emerged from their daytime forms: eyes, all-seeing, searched for the moon, silently scrutinised the sky for the slightest hint of anything suspicious, sniffed the dusk, then hopped through the sharp stubble, unhurt. Soon the pyramids of corn would be harvested and the stubble set alight to burn as witches whose spirits returned to wander the earth as brown hares. With tension coiled and tightly sprung, the hares bounded past the sweeping and swooping swallows, fearfully.

When the scene before us dimmed with the growing night, Nature became eyeless, then faceless, then shapeless. My mind struggled on the brink of reason as daytime outlines became unsound and suspect and melted hideously into the dusk. Deep down in my soul, dark fright was fermenting and fighting back a primeval scream. With hearts seeped in superstition, we sped home.

We dare not linger by the bridge now, and peer over the parapet at the burn some twenty feet below. That was a daytime activity when life was casual and cheeky and impudent as an infant. Time held no meaning then – we might spend two minutes looking over the bridge, or twelve, or not look over at all. But we were always drawn there as blood pulled up a syringe, and the burn flowed rhythmically under the bridge like blood in our veins; and we checked it like we would our pulse – the stronger the spate, the better we felt.

But we could not stop to reassure ourselves now. Not in the darkening, when vision was guesswork tinged with dread. Dread of bogeymen and dreams turned sour. Dread of 'the Hand' which lurked under the bridge at night, and could appear, I shouldn't wonder, like an ugly troll, to grab even the quietest tiptoer. Fear was in the burn and in our veins and flowed freely in through useless eyes.

An unexpected shower could now fall, even a downpour, but we would not crouch, now, under an umbrella of branches, hunched on our heels like old stiff Cossack dancers, until muscles ached and midges bit a bandeau of blood-red beads on our foreheads, and all the while unseen pixies sniggered and catapulted raindrops at each other above our heads, and beyond rain would stream down like stair rods. No, not now, in the gloom, would we shelter.

Blackness loomed loftily above us and came after us with outstretched arms. We pulled our duffel coats tightly around us. I moved closer to Margaret and tried to echo her footsteps on the hard road. Between each step there was a timeless pause, before I heard my other boot touch the road. I willed my boots to be limpet-boots which sucked the road so that nothing could prise me off. But the deliberation and energy needed to place my limpet-boots on the road slowed me down, appallingly. All around us the pelting rain quickened and raced as heavy hooves, chasing. Above us, the night was a black velvet cloak of infinite length which flapped and billowed above us, threatening to ensnare us like a trawler's net. Perhaps we were already swimming to the dead end, and were minutes away from the ultimate fright?

Our hopes were pinned on a square of yellow light which twinkled and beckoned from the side window of the Lodge, like a lighthouse. There lay our only promise of comfort and respite. Every cell in our bodies focused furiously on that light and we battered towards it like suicidal moths. On and on endlessly, until at last, the solid door of the Lodge was slammed on imps and demons. I leaned against its weight, momentarily, to allow the light and warmth of the fire to soothe and clothe me from head to toe in a delicious, diaphanous drape of relief! I spooned in that feeling like double cream until I was bloated with excess, then I followed Margaret into the front room and joined the light and laughter in front of the fire.

As the autumn enchantment wore on, swallows strung themselves on power lines like ebony beads, motionless, but making an almighty din. Raucous like squabbling children, arguing, they clung quarrelling to their lines. Nothing and nobody could be unaware of their intention to leave the coolness and migrate somewhere like Africa. Everything and everyone concluded, 'The sooner the better'. But each summer, everyone would again be enchanted by their return and welcome their flightiness, their speed, their keenness of eye, their quick-wittedness, their elegance and their sheer devil-may-care attitude. And if anyone had asked me then, what I'd like to be when I grew up, I'd surely have replied, without hesitation, 'A swallow'.

By October, drab, sapless, hitherto-green leaves became vermilion and gold, and braes of bracken became crisply russet, dotted in between with shiny-red rosehips and bunches of rowan berries. Some years the blackberries were jet-black, fat and juicy while other years they wouldn't darken until November. But after October they had 'the devil's spit on them' and were hard, sour and bitter.

Up the Strath, hazel kernels ripened and clusters of eight, or even nine, nuts could be found in the topmost branches. But even if we retrieved hoards of these like greedy squirrels, once we'd cracked these mega-clusters open with a flat stone, we'd discover that the nuts inside were minute compared to the more plentiful, easier to reach, clusters of two; and sometimes, disappointingly, there was only dust inside them.

Just before the cold set in with determination and before the wind ripped all the dead-skin leaves from twigs and branches, leaving them as visible skeletons with bloodless veins and capillaries, there were always three, or four, almost summery days which gave a brief respite from cold death. Oddly, butterflies were temporarily revived into a fluttering, like falling leaves; and half-dead wasps dozily idled indoors looking not for food, but a victim to sting.

Crazed with this final longing, they settled on tea towels, on

coat lapels, on taps, amongst the clothes pegs, anywhere, silently hoping for an unsuspecting hand to cover them, while quietly humming, 'If only, if only, if only.' Sizzling bluebottles came from somewhere, to buzz in threes and fours at inside window panes, or formed a club on a sunny front door, or attacked light bulbs, kamikaze-fashion, in the evening, impervious to pain, anxious for an end.

Mushrooms and fungi erupted from the ground and from rotting trees, like acne. However edible some could be, we wouldn't touch them. We didn't know their names. They were all 'toadstools', warty like toads, and we were sure that the devil had something to do with them. They lived in rottenness like maggots. A fairy ring of fungi in Nana's lawn was trodden down instinctively. Derek would kick puffballs in the Shore Park to smithereens of dust, but I skirted round them and pretended not to notice them growing more monstrous each weekend.

Rowan trees protected country folk from witches. Their saplings grew easily in the spring and in some unlikely places, like the sides of dykes and in mossy rone pipes. Unnoticed, they sprouted in gardens between roses, but left to grow, they reached a height when it would be unlucky to pull them out. Even today, in one Caithness village, there remains a rowan tree growing right in front of the living-room window of a council house. It must prevent daylight entering, but a series of tenants have preferred to move house, rather than cut it down.

Old folk commented on the plumpness of the rowan berry – if it had ripened to ruby earlier than usual; the exact shading of the red – and with that knowledge which old folk have, would conclude, 'Aye . . . it's going to be a hard winter'. And it was. But then, I don't recall a winter that wasn't long and hard. How revered the rowan was! But we did not pick and eat, or bottle and retain, those berries of wisdom. Instead, starlings slipped into speckled waistcoats and like magicians made them disappear in a flash.

When Hallowe'en came, it was nearly always a school night in

Thurso and not, thank goodness, a weekend night in Latheron-wheel, where the Lodge was a long, dark half-mile from the houses in the village. In a Thurso orange with street lights, me and Carinda dressed up as witches, practised a joke or two, lit the red candles in our neepie lanterns, and then pulled down our cardboard masks over our faces.

We went from door to door until we collected a week's supply of sweets, a harvest of fruit, a monkey's delight of nuts and enough coins to count into satisfying towers. Then, when our bags got embarrassingly heavy because of our greed; when our masks (which were by no means an exact copy of where our eyes and mouth actually were, and were made in Hong Kong for Chinese children) became irritatingly inexact and warm inside with our breath; when we tired of repeating the same jokes over and over again, until they were no longer funny; when we passed groups of masked, sniggering guisers whom we thought

we knew but weren't sure; and when my neepie lantern began to
dim and on lifting the lid I noticed first the stench of cooking
swede, and then that the red candle was a bloody sea of wax; and
when the street lighting seemed to flicker on and off – then, we
said our goodbyes and each rushed home for a better look at our
spoils in a bright white light. Not bad for one night's witching!

November the fifth soon followed and with it came a boxful
of jumping jacks, a Catherine wheel, about two Roman candles,
four or five rockets and a few sparklers. It was a visual and aural
delight on a sharp dark night at the Lodge. I was wrapped in
many layers of heavy clothing, stamping my feet and clapping
my hands to warm my merriment. And everyone was clouded in
comic-book speech-bubbles of wordless dragon's breath. My
blocked nose would now start to pour as my mittened hands
fumbled up my sleeve and in my pockets for that already damp
hankie. Or else, I'd try to hold my breath to stop a tickly cough,
which, once started, would persist on and on until my whole
body was obsessed with it and could concentrate on nothing
else. Winter, lurking around me, then laid a cold hand on my
shoulder and patted my back. But that few minutes of fireworks
was a delight which couldn't be missed and coughs and colds
were commonplace.

Everyone and everything was winding down to winter. That
spontaneous, short-sleeved, sunny joy, that vivid-greenness was
dying in dark crumpled bundles under bare bushes. It would be
a long time till Christmas.

7

Rain, Sun, Moon and Stars

Sometimes it would rain non-stop for three days more than the ground could cope with. Then the land lay sodden like an overwet bath sponge, oozing with water and mud and a lingering dampness which clung like an uncomfortably tight, shrunken jumper round everyone and everything. On such sombre days we sat around with dull expressions, feeling morose. Margaret, Derek and I niggled and moaned grudgingly at each other – for each knew the others found pleasure in it.

On such a day nothing went right: any project we'd start would be doomed by impatience; any book we'd idly pick up would be boring, any daydream would be flat and stale; any adult advice would be unvaried and petty – in short, a day which we longed to pull our arms out of and throw in a quick pile on the floor and leave behind in sleep. But the day had only just begun, Time teased and poked with a sharp, prodding finger.

Mam always found things to do. I followed her around, lingering like the dampness, becoming an annoying shadow, but not really meaning to: getting in the way, nearly being stood on, and then impatiently tutted at. Mam could spend a good half-hour scuttering about in the dim coal shed, breaking boulders of coal with a hammer, thudding them into smaller chunks and filling three or four pails with these odd-sized shapes. Then with a small hatchet, she divided logs, which pinged on the flagstone floor, into even-sized kindling.

All the while the rain resonated on the corrugated iron roof like a percussion crescendo. I could stand there, watching her, or turn my back on her and gaze through the open door at a glaucoma of greyness, of sky and land blurring and merging and

blurring again. The soil was pounded smooth by the thumping
rain.

'What are ye standing there for? Away ye go into the warmness. There's no sense in getting cowld,' Mam said, head down,
neatening the sticks into a pile. She was right. There was no
point. There was nothing to see.

I wished a flock of redwings would alight on the grass and
bob about for an easy picking of worms. But my eyes saw
nothing, just infinite gloom. I went slowly back to the door of
the Lodge, ignoring the rain and dragging my feet, hopeful for a
last-minute distraction, but if there was one, it was beyond my
sight. I struggled to make out a scuffling beetle, or other small
insects, on the edge of my hearing . . . Meanwhile Mam followed
heavily at my back, laden with two zinc pails of coal. 'Come on.
A bit faster.'

The fire was banked up and a few tattie peelings thrown at the back to make the coal last, for it was going to be a long day. Mam threw our coats on a peg, washed her hands and picked up her knitting needles from the floor at the side of her chair. I listened to the click-clacking of pins and the sizzling fire splutter.

Being momentarily stuck there in vagueness, my mind in some slow, drugged, drowsy state, I was inveigled into winding a ball of wool with Nana. Rather, she wound the ball while my arms mechanically held the tension in the hank. I longed to be the winder as my outstretched arms ached and my eyes tired of watching the yarn and twisting my hand just as the wool reached it, so that the rhythm of the winder was not snagged. A small, quite round, tight ball was the result.

Knitting continued in an easy rhythm, the coals calmed and conversation resumed. The adults were settled for the afternoon. As the hours passed, jumpers grew into recognisable shapes, or heels of socks were turned neatly from memory. Probably any garment could be knitted. Nana told us that her sister had knitted fingered gloves and backed them with rabbit fur which she, herself, had prepared. (In Nana's childhood, before the introduction of myxomatosis, every family snared wild rabbits for stew.)

We were like primitives, I thought, huddled round a flame, making clothes from patterns handed down from memory, by generations before. Three generations sat together and I knew I was unconsciously being taught to wind and knit, also. But I didn't want to sit still and learn. I wanted, instead, to be out and away in a wood, or sheltering like a bird on a cliff ledge. Alert. Watching. Waiting with nerves coiled and tightly sprung. Listening.

But the day stretched out in a click, clack, tick, tock rhythm and the rain just would not pause, even slightly, to allow me to declare loudly, 'It's stopped!' And then bolt out on an adventure, anywhere in the stinking soddenness.

Even Mam would have been relieved to agree to such an

outing, to get some peace to knit with that gay, satisfying rhythm which made garments grow. Instead I sat and fidgeted and narked, much like a damp stick thrown on the fire which spluttered and sparked and splintered onto the mat, singeing another hole. Sometimes I would stamp it out before it burned and sometimes I would pretend not to notice and left it to burn, to see what shape it made in the red nylon mat.

I went to bed in bad humour. It was another wasted day. I cast off that clinging-jumper-of-a-day, with its row on row of boredom which I had knitted, and left it in the pile of clothes at the bottom of my bed, and hoped it would not be there in the morning. Even as I closed my eyes, the rain relentlessly lashed at the skylight and penetrated my dreamtime, curdling any last-minute chance of an imaginary thrilling adventure. It was a bitter lullaby.

Many a weekend was wasted on such days of forced imprison-ment and repetitive depression. After a spell of these days, it would have been effortless to have become a pagan sun-worshipper and to have thought that age-old superstitions could well be sensible and reasonable, and could well have had more than a grain of truth in them. That Caithness is, indeed, a distance from the heart of Scotland and thrust out from it like a fist, clenched against the lash of the elements, yet furled round superstition as holding the answer to many an inexplicable mystery.

Pagan worship of the sun, for example, was reasonable to a crofter whose whole life depended on the sun's whims to warm the soil and induce and nourish the green shoot of life into crops – especially before state subsidies, which many proud old-folk found difficult to accept. Then praise be to the sun! It lightened many a heart and brought a spontaneous smile which revived the wrinkles on shrunken, rain-weathered faces.

In an inhospitable county like Caithness with a wretched soil and a meaner climate – where crofters scraped a living with one cow, a handful of sheep, a dozen hens, a strip of land and a bank of peat somewhere – luck was important. A 'stroke of luck' was a significant bonus and not to be scoffed at. Bad luck could be the final breaking-point for many a soul, clinging by his fingertips to the edge of existence.

In that case, was it really superstitious nonsense to keep one black sheep in a flock, for good luck? After all, if a flock of white Cheviots was protected by having one black sheep, then there was no extra effort in having one, just to be sure. Was that believing in superstition, or merely common sense?

And if a female neighbour was suspected of having 'the evil eye', there was a risk in showing her a sickly ewe, in case the aforementioned beast died. It would, therefore, be more neighbourly not to show her an ill animal, just in case. Many remembered Bell Royal, whom many feared as a witch, and who had lived in a remote hut near the Bell Tower in Latheron. Out of spite, she had put a spell on a crofter's cow and killed it.

After a bout of wet days, a dull mind could imagine much and think it true. A mind was prone to irrationality and a body prone to ageing stiffness. Despair could set in with evil intent. But wake up to a crisp autumn day, with just a cool sun, and a mind could bounce freshly back like a healthy infant. The grey, heavy damask curtain of rainclouds was pulled back from in front of our eyes to reveal soft, fuzzy voile thumbprints in a frail duck-egg sky. Ripples of geese, changing their 'V' shape like an artist's quick charcoal sketch, would billow blaringly south.

The miracle of sight restored! Stale apathy was now expurgated much like moisture was whipped from a sagging washing line of heavy, white cotton sheets, when they were made to flap like flags and crack horizontal by a smacking gale straight off the sea. Once dry, two people held adjacent corners, lent back and pulled against each other to ensure that there were fewer creases for the last traces of apathy to hide in. The clean white sheets were then brought indoors and the house was scented by their sweet freshness.

Eyes can pick out subtle nuances in our immediate surroundings and I had come to rely on their responses to what I saw: the edges, the shapes, the colour, the shadows – but they were, in fact, a poor recorder of truth when great distances were involved. They were deceived when they saw the slow movement of a silent jet on the tip of a vapour trail, beyond sound, with its course set straight to infinity. For eyes cannot perceive the Infinite.

On a clear, frosty autumn night, the sky is a chickenpox of gleaming constellations. On such a night, Margaret and I would take it in turns to shine a torch on one of the dot drawings in my *Observer's Book of Astronomy*, while the other gazed upwards to locate Orion, Cassiopeia, Taurus, Perseus, The Great Bear and all the others. While looking for Auriga, high overhead, we lost our balance and fell backwards into a ditch! How we laughed at our foolishness in full view of the Universe. Embarrassed, we went home. Once inside the Lodge, I read the chunks of text between each diagram and my comprehension of what I'd seen outside was dull.

My eyes had been deceived by the two-dimensional picture in the sky. The brightest star, Sirius, was probably the nearest but by no means the biggest. The biggest, from what I could gather, was Epsilon Aurigae, near Capella, which has a diameter of two thousand million miles, yet is quite insignificant to the naked eye. Rigel, in Orion, is fifty thousand times more luminous than the sun and is nine hundred light years away, which meant that we saw it as it was nine hundred years ago. Instantly, we had looked back in time. I read about the immense distances, timespans and temperatures. Even the colours of stars trick the naked eye: the red stars are not hot, but cool, and the white/blue stars are not cool, but hot. And when my brain struggled with the concept of millions and millions, I read that through Andromeda there is another galaxy, beyond ours, with distances in excess of the billions that I had tried to understand.

I snapped the book shut. Then my eyes would remain 'naked' – naked as an uncivilised, ignorant, superstitious native. I went to the front door of the Lodge and looked up, calmly and reason-ably, at the stars in the same place in the sky (yet moving beyond

my sight) in a final attempt to understand the distances involved.
Immediately I was aware that mud was seeping through the blue
velour tops of my slippers and that my feet were getting cold.
There was a chill in the air. Again I looked up at a rash of stars but
cared not that 'neighbouring' stars were actually six million,
million miles apart. My feet were in the mud and I was worried
about the scolding I might get for dirtying my good slippers.

I smiled at my brain toying with the 'native' solution. I
thought back to when Derek and I ran around, me in my
knickers and liberty bodice, and Derek bare to his pants, each
with crow feathers stuck down the side of our bandannas, and
we were Red Indian braves, playing in the sun. At that time, I
neither cared nor knew that the sun was 92.9 million miles away
from Earth. 'Sun' rhymed with 'fun' and 'run' and not with 'star'
and 'far'. It was just there in the morning when we opened the
curtains, like a huge football, beckoning us to come and play.

We drew crayon pictures of a round yellow sun, its rays spoked
evenly like a cartwheel in a two-inch band of bright blue, high-
up sky. Four blank inches below, standing on the two-inch band
of green grass, were happy children playing. Children, smiling
straight at the observer, with their hair drawn vertically above
their heads – for, how else could a four-year-old artist show that
children had long hair? Back view would show no face, and
therefore no expression, and side views were too difficult to
contemplate. Face-to-face portraits were the most rewarding, the
most meaningful. Hair, then, could only be vertical.

We drew unhappy children sometimes – we weren't stupid.
We knew people weren't always ecstatic. But if the sun was in
our pictures, smiling on high, then the people we'd drawn were
guaranteed to be smiling also. It was just a fact. The Infinite was
as important in the scheme of my earthly life at four as a broken
wax crayon unconsciously flicked into flight between my thumb
and fingernail.

I was carefree in my ignorance then. Within a twenty-five-
mile radius of Latheronwheel was my life. A sixty-mile round

trip to visit relatives in Brora was a day trip; an outing to Inverness, over a hundred miles away, was a holiday! Like Nana always said, it was nice to go away for a change, but then, so especially nice to be home again – like putting on a favourite pair of slippers with the soft rubber insole moulded into the exact shape of each toe. Coming home was, then, a skin-slipper so perfect, so comfortable, so relaxing. So safe to be home again and slip so easily into the same routine. To close my eyes and in my mind picture the village of Latheronwheel, with its sun-washed cottages, strung like white bunting to the braehead of the Shore. Then, to round the corner at Knockinnon and see it for real, was such a welcome sight!

But now in the dark it was different. There was nothing to see but the Infinite. How far was Heaven then? Beyond Andromeda? That rash, that chickenpox of stars overhead became a discomfort and itched at my brain. My eyes could make no sense of it, either half-open or fully open. They divided the sky into quadrilaterals, rhombuses and parallelograms, all as flat as pancakes.

I had no comprehension of space, time or distance. I felt stupid and peeved to feel it. To ignore the Infinite was the only solution. Ignorance was indeed bliss and I soothed it over my itchy brain, like Calamine Lotion, and it cooled and calmed it temporarily.

Meantime, eyes could still be trusted to recognise nearer, more tangible events which were more intimate and therefore part of something familiar. The Infinite was too scary. It was plucked out of a black nightmare of vast dimensions which the brain had wrestled in vain to make sense of. It was lumpy and slimy, with piercing white eyes of great magnitude. I just wanted to scream out, so that I could be comforted and told softly that it didn't matter and that I'd feel better in the morning. But I knew about it now. I'd read the details and couldn't forget. The darkness made me feel uneasy anyway, but dwelling on the Infinite mixed with the darkness made me feel extra frightened and insecure. Oh, to be four again and so able to easily forget!

Next morning, the sun had erased the stars again with a luminous splendid sparkle. Despair and darkness evaporated. Praise be to the sun – the confidence-builder!

Looking down from space, I was nothing a speck, or perhaps an insignificant amoeba. Yet, in Latheronwheel, that place then unmarked on a map of Britain, a place which didn't exist for strangers, a nowhere place which only maybe existed in dreams, I tramped the daytime land of Picts and Vikings, proudly and fearlessly, with a lilt in my step and a glint in my eye for adventure.

And if a spaceship from a far-flung planet had landed in the Shore Park, during the day, I would neither have been astonished nor frightened, because Latheronwheel seemed a place where anything could happen, but nothing was more unlikely. Nothing unusual ever occurred. But skim below the humdrum and the mundane, the shallowness of landscape and greyness of weather, and there was energy and humour and life and nature exposed in their rawness. With an active imagination or a keen, near-focused eye, you could add tinsel and glitter to many an experience and make it memorable.

8

Mad Dogs and Seadogs

Budding adventurers found it more exciting to go down to the Shore than up the Strath. The Strath was pretty and heady with scented flowers – a feminine walk which enticed the senses, but going to the Shore was thrilling, more hazardous to an explorer and more boyish.

Depending on our stamina and inclination, we could seek out hidden shores like Cleishgag, some twenty minutes away from the village, by heading north on top of the cliffs. From the sheep-trodden path we could view the ragged Caithness coastline with its stacks set out from the cliffs like dry teetering sandcastles, and seagulls gliding effortlessly by like nylon kites.

But the journey to Cleishgag was through many fields and tiring, and if the tide was in, there were no rock pools to explore and nothing extra to lure an adventurer. The Shore at Latheronwheel held much more, was closer at hand and gave a choice of three ways to reach it.

Firstly, it was possible to travel with the burn downstream straight to the harbour, but only on easy summer days when the water was low and belonged to the white-shirted dippers which bobbed in and under it. The boulders dotted along its length then were exposed jumping-stones. But after heavy rain – the burn swelled into a wide, brown peaty serpent which gushed and galloped zigzag to the sea, levelling the angled boulders below its surface and bringing branches and leaves hurtling along its cream-spiked back. Its roar and speed were frightening. We could only stop, look and listen, but not cross.

To beat a path along the riverbank was always an option, but we would have to battle through barbed brambles, which was, frankly, more maddening than thrilling. However, Derek seemed to delight in whacking through the brambles with a stick. Perhaps that was a boy's idea of an adventure. Derek assumed leadership. He had the stick.

To follow him closely as leader usually meant we had to be sharp-witted, to avoid bramble and tree branches being sprung suddenly into our faces, as Derek elbowed and hacked his way bravely to the Shore. Derek was a competent hero, but always in such a hurry. He seemed to have the burn in him. He could not wait and worry about the whimpering behind him, as he let go of another branch, which arrowed straight at my forehead, while I had quickly glanced down at the deep mud at my feet and the clump of nettles waiting silently to my left. The pain in my head and the side of my nose smarted as I staggered left ways, of course, into the nettles. There were no dock leaves. Margaret muttered some words of comfort, while Derek shouted, 'Scaredy-calfies' from far out in front somewhere. He couldn't stop. He flailed and flowed forever forwards towards the Shore.

But we girls would stick together and choose another of the two remaining routes to the Shore. The second was through the Shore Park, where we had seen the black rabbit. Following the tractor path and leaping every four-foot-high thistle alongside, it was possible to reach the braehead in five minutes or so. Then, it was just a case of going through the turnstile gate down the slope to the old, grassy, arched bridge over the burn and then follow on to the Shore.

The third was to go through the village. The shops and the Hotel, called 'the Blends', were clumped together at the top of the road to the Shore. Opposite Kemp's shop, on the other side of the main road and up on a hill, was the dark manse with a collar of trees round it. It was bigger than the Big House and towered above the village and surrounding crofts. Below it, a field away, was a row of terraced cottages, and in one of them lived the watchmaker. I forget his name, but I can't forget his clocks. Some were stopped, some ticked gently and skipped lightly through the hours, some had bonny faces and delicate chimes, while others simply plodded out a mechanical beat, like a weary labourer's boots.

On one of the walls was a print of the painting by W. F. Yeames, entitled, 'And When Did You Last See Your Father?' It shows a small, straight-backed, proud, honest boy being questioned by a parliamentary officer during the Civil War. His mother and older sister are in tears in the background and, closer to him, his younger sister is openly weeping. Soldiers fill the room, but they appear friendly, which is all part of their deception.

Yeames painted everyone and everything in similar dowdy colours but the small boy, alone, was painted in bright blue clothes. All eyes are on little boy blue, and so were mine. To save his father's life he must lie. But he looks so honest! What will he reply? What would I have said? I stared hypnotically at the boy. In that room in Latheronwheel, where Time was beating out at various hours in confusing rhythms, there was an aching hiatus . . .

I heard no clocks. Time stopped. The boy's answer was now my responsibility. What did I think he would say? A man's life depended on it. And I was there in that picture. I felt the tension. I smelt the fear. But the boy just wouldn't move his lips to reply. The painting just would not come to life to act out the next vital seconds. Please just his reply – for on knowing that the rest would be obvious. Many clocks chimed the hour. I was back in my shoes. Many cogs from many wheels turned Time forever forwards, but the tension remained in a time long past, in an unforgettable picture which shows that childlike honesty could be devastating and not always the best policy that adults said it was.

Next to Kemp's was the Church Hall, the Blends and then Maclean's General Store. There were only two shops. The Post Office, the churches and the school were a mile away in Latheron. The main county towns of Wick and Thurso were both about twenty miles away, in different directions. So village folk and crofters depended on vans to provide butcher meat, fish and bread.

Occasionally dark-skinned traders came with suitcases selling clothes, linen, brushes, polish and pegs, promising good luck with all sales. 'Johnny-Inghan' came from France on his bike, it was said, selling strings of onions round the houses. It was the only time I ever met a person with a different colour of skin and a strange accent when I was young.

Equally fascinating was taking shoes to Robert-the-shoe-maker. His hut was just below Maclean's. It was tiny but full of cobbler paraphernalia. Even as Robert spoke softly to us as he worked, my eyes were once more drawn seductively away from his craft and conversation towards the wildcat skin, stretched out on the wall above his head. The animal was of no great size but its nose was curled to reveal yellow fangs – an expression of menace or fear.

Margaret and I had come across two, in different parts of the wood. One had run off into the rushes and we merely saw its stripy tail, while the other backed into a tree stump and showed its teeth as we walked past. They both looked like feral tomcats. They were more scared of us than we were of them. They posed no threat to us. But adults obviously held a different opinion of them: to them they were trophies. Stuck forever with its teeth showing, the skinned wildcat did seem scary, the longer I stared at it.

Beyond the shops and amenities at the top of the village, a chain of cottages were linked to the Shore road. Nana knew all the folk in the village and they knew us as 'Mrs Donn's grandchildren'. Sometimes old women, heading for the shops with straw shopping bags, would smile 'Hello' or question us out of curiosity, or for gossip. Or women in print aprons would round the corners of their homes, banging the side of a zinc pail of mash, calling hens to dinner. They wouldn't oblige us to stop and talk, thank goodness. They would merely wave or shout a greeting. We didn't even mind the quiver of net curtains as we passed – rather that than be delayed from rounding the corner of the brae and, at last, be out of sight of every house in the village. Only then could we be ourselves, or else boys, and behave as impolitely as we liked. We turned left at the bottom of the hill and met up with the burn, running like us to the Shore.

The cliffs bend round Latheronwheel harbour in a semi-circle like an old man's torso, with two solid arms of quays curved round, embracing three or four lobster boats which bobbed about brightly and confidently on a summer's day. Thrown on the 'arms' were nets, drying, and piles of creels made of hazelwood, waiting to be baited for crabs and lobsters.

Summer was time to take advantage of the leeside of the cliffs and picnic in the sheltered field below them, much to the amusement of Robert's dozen or so sheep, which grazed there. They arrogantly stared at us and back at each other, to check that they all shared the same opinion: that we were trespassing on their property. Even the black sheep agreed. But once the communal thought had been shared, it passed silently by and they took no further action. Faintly embarrassed by their own indifference, they began to graze, walking slowly but consciously,

away from us, as if they cared not a hoot if we stayed or not. But I knew if I took two steps towards them, lifted my arms and shouted a greeting, genuine like 'Good afternoon', or gobbledy-gook like 'Oohaaah', they would take to their stupid heels, ears back, great jelly-bellies wobbling on thin branches of legs, all together, in an exodus of fear. But that was not my intention.

Instead, Margaret passed the lemonade bottle to me. I lifted it to my lips, head back, slurped, wiped my mouth on the back of my hand boyishly, screwed on the stopper and left it behind a shady tussock with my socks and sandals. Next we painfully made a path over the dusty, gritty road and onto the beach.

It was full of boulders and coloured shingle of sea-polished rock and sea-polished glass – the colours more intense when wet and quite unremarkable when dry. The sea lapped gently and rhythmically onto the exposed boulders as the tide went out. It was some sport leaping quickly from one uneven boulder to the next. It was a test of nimbleness between brain and foot and, if our co-ordination was wrong and we misjudged the slipperiness of the slime on the next stone, then the consequences were painful bruises to our shins.

Even in summer, the shallow water was icy. The shingle and exposed buckies were sharp underfoot. But we found feathery green, orange and red delicate petticoats of seaweed floating just under the surface of the water. (We once took these home to float in a basin of tap water; but there their beauty was stopped still, dead somehow; their beauty had been their motion in the sea.) When our feet became too cold, we stepped backwards onto a sun-warmed boulder, which acted momentarily as a hotwater bottle, and we repeated the sequence again and again.

When we eventually retrieved our socks and sandals and brushed away the final bits of shingle, which clung like buckies to the cracks in our curled-up feet, it was blissful to stretch on our socks and feel our feet tingle with warmth, and then to flatten them comfortably onto our sandal soles. With a last swig of lemonade apiece, Margaret took the empty bottle to the water's edge and tossed it in. We could spend ten minutes or so, firing pebbles at it, overhand and underhand, little caring whether our aim was good or not, but smirking proudly if we hit it, nonetheless.

The sun was high in the heavens, our stomachs were full, the sea sparkled gently and God smiled above us and we were in His embrace. We lingered looking for small crabs under stones at the sea line and watched little beasties jump as we exposed them to the light, but soon we left the harbour, crossed the bridge and returned home to the Lodge, via the Shore Park.

That arched bridge across the burn is wide and the thoroughfare is now full of weeds, but it was the route reputed to have been taken by stagecoaches to reach the village, ages ago. Indeed, the village is so named because the stagecoaches had to brake on the steep incline and someone slammed a pad of leather on the wheels – hence, 'Leather-on-wheel', as Latheronwheel is locally pronounced. Mam told me that story, and I choose to believe it.

Many a yarn is told in homes, or in the Blends, of how the upturned half of a boat, the *King William*, came to be under the cliffs at the harbour to form an umbrella-like structure. My Uncle Sandy told me how two men had equal shares in the boat. However, the fishing had been poor for many years and one man approached the other in the Blends and asked for his half-share back. The other replied, greatly aided by whisky, that he could take his half of the boat if he liked, but his own half was returning with him to Lybster. Thereupon, his partner made his way back to the harbour with a saw, and cut the boat in half. Once this task was complete, he returned to the bar and told the other that the latter's half was ready to sail to Lybster, whenever he could manage it! When the drunk man learnt what had happened, he laughed and laughed. Whether the story is true or not, one half of the boat remained, intact, at the harbour until recently, when it succumbed to the drying sun and lashings of stormy weather because the harbour was not always a tranquil and blissful place.

Even in early autumn, a change could be felt in the wind sneaking round the jetty. There was spite and malice in it. The waves curled into the harbour and snarled, showing white teeth.

Beyond, the bottle-green sea was marled granite with white breakers snapping and snatching at cliff, or sea bird, or boat, or harbour wall, like a savage dog, crazed. The wind, its invisible accomplice, wooshed and swirled like a demented demon, whipping waves to swoosh over the breakwater.

It was a game to run to and fro on the pier, trying to time these huge spits of saltwater and dashing in between them. However, the ground was soon awash, uneven and now slippery, and to concentrate on our footing was at the expense of our run. Eventually we'd both get caught and with heavy drenched duffel coats we'd shelter under the *King William*. Squinting through cracks, we saw seagulls flung into confusion like paper aeroplanes. Funnily enough, there was always one diving bird, dipping under the waves in the storm-filled harbour, perfectly happy, while turmoil spilled around it.

The small boats twisted and strained on their moorings as great suds of foam from rabid jaws were cast onto the beach and were then blown about in the gale. If we stood out in it, feet apart and braced against its fierceness, the foam swarmed and stuck to our dark duffel coats like a sponge and we became snowmen.

But the air was salty, bitter and numbing with a viciousness that was not winter and its nostalgic jolliness, but a clawing, scratching, blood-red rawness that only fishermen knew and had come to respect. For we were just children who patted the sleeping dog in the sunshine and were uncertain and frightened when it turned its head and bared its teeth. Its hackles rose and stretched out to the ocean. They curved and dipped, not like porpoises in a summer sea, but haphazardly, with no pattern, in wildness. We turned out of the biting wind and with red-whipped faces went sheepishly home.

And the sea relentlessly gnawed and clawed at the shingle, pulling great weights of it down and up, roaring and rolling and crashing to the very heart of the cliff. But the arms of the quays held firm at the leash and once more contained it, but never hoped to tame it.

While brave fishermen lapped beer and whisky in the warmth of the Blends, relatives could be out there, lashed to the wheel, heading for port. To arrive safely or to perish, both were accepted equally, for a man could know the lie of the rocks and the neighbourhood in which he fished but he was not so arrogant as to know the sea, its muzzled ferocity, its freakish waves. God's name could be uttered through bloody oaths of fear, or gently in compassionate prayer, but He could not answer, He would not answer. His will would be done, whatever. Besides, none could swim. None would survive the bitter coldness if they could. Live or die, this was their job, their life, or death. Many a man, on safely reaching the harbour, again left God drying in the nets while he flirted with the demon drink in the pub. A demon which caressed cold bones, stroked smiles onto flushed faces and encouraged talk from the shyest man.

Was this fun, or sin? Why did God choose a fisherman as a disciple – they who sat, godless, in coarse jerseys with coarse

talk, fondling a nip. All the while their wives hummed hymns and neatened homes with God around them like a warm perfume. With a spirit thus raised, wives knitted diligently, in good humour, but the scent soon soured when they heard the steady masculine thump of boots on the flagstone path outside, and the slow deliberate hand on the latch.

Then many a wife let loose an unchristian fury with a relentless devilish tongue, cold and savage and heartless as the worst sea. The female tirade continued in waves and crashed in their ears, coldly and pitilessly, while they silently steered a concentrated course to some harbour – a cold bed, if they were lucky. There they lowered their heads and never dared to stretch a casual hand over to the warm space where wives and God lay together.

With the holy light of a hushed Sabbath, some fishermen awoke, deaf to the monotonous 'dong, dong' of the bell in the church tower, calling all to worship. Perhaps they felt too unworthy or too embarrassed to go to church. As wives prepared to meet God in their best coats and best hats, already humming hymns while powdering their noses and then attending to stubborn flecks of dust on their coats with the backs of their hands, these fishermen, in overalls and cloth caps and a haze of tobacco, would skulk around in outhouses, glad of the peace and cover they provided, and mumble excuses through pipe-sucking mouths.

Yet, they who felt so unworthy, would help anyone who asked for aid, in any task, with a gladness that didn't require recompense and with a warmness more long-lasting than whisky. The deep 'dong, dong' could cut at a conscience with a clear sharp note like a calm sea, flat as a mill pond, still as a mirror. Men would look seaward and scan the coastline of Banff, some forty miles away, blurred and furry at the edges, but a revelation nonetheless. It lightened the spirit like a friendly arm around the shoulder and brought a faint smile to their lips and a thoughtful suck at their pipes. The ocean was asleep, its coat silky-smooth and shining, peaceful now. Fishermen knew of its wicked white-of-eye that bairns would do well to heed and be cautious of.

But we were immature, boyish and reckless. On summer days and sun days, we climbed down narrow sheep-worn slopes into steep gullies, bitten out of the cliffs. Down there were massive chunks of rock, flat as tables, longer than trawler decks and higher than a child's shoulders. Chests flattened against the cliff, feet and fingers had to feel out narrow ledges for footholds, while the sea gurgled through deep crevices, like a gulping killer whale. Once reached, these secret places echoed eerily with the screaming of startled gulls. The boulders here were giant cannonballs. Stuck in between were flotsam and smooth driftwood, remains of seabirds and always the carcass of one dead sheep.

Attached to the rocks were clumps of air-filled sachets of seaweed which made the most pleasurable sound when jumped on, like bubble wrap today. Further along these rocks, nearer the sea, were ribbons of seaweed floating with the waves like flowing, twenty-four-inch-long octopus tentacles. This was the tangle we were looking for. After a storm this kind was washed into the harbour and, if we were lucky, we would find a fresh piece to eat. Here it was extra fresh and still stuck to the rock.

We ripped off and discarded the thin, flat slimy strips from either side of the fleshy, salty, narrow brown stem. This was the only kind of tangle we ate. Mam said it was good for us. Indeed, she had given us lengths of it, as teething babies. Here in this hidden store it was more plentiful and more long-lasting than a liquorice strap.

On a summer's day with a piercing sun, we ran along the gully over massive rocks, like prehistoric reptiles, with our brown, tangle-tongues dangling. On such a day, in such a place, I looked upon a pre-man landscape – a time of chunks and boulders and roughness. Shapes of pterodactyls skimmed off the cliffs above and I stood stone-still against a rock and bit my tongue. But only fulmars flew over me.

The rocks could be a boat, or a whale's back. If we scaled the

'deck' or 'back', and searched long enough, we'd always find a perfect rock-chair to sit on and lean into and so look out on a distant glittering sea, as waves lapped a happy beat way below our feet. I closed my eyes. A coloured piercing kaleidoscope of odd shapes danced hypnotically inside my eyelids, as the sun continued to beat down . . . The sound of the tide, slinking in snatches, niggled like a spoilsport at that warm drifting feeling of a fleeting dream.

My ears just would not relax. Now the seagulls' cries seemed louder with a pricking sharpness which made me sit up and look. The motionless shags on the faraway rocks now silently spread their wings like black tattered sheets to dry. The dark rocks below felt suddenly hard. The 'gloop-gloop' of the water seemed closer and colder to my dangling ankles. It would be careless to stay longer.

'The tide's coming in fast. We'd better go,' said Margaret. We scrambled towards the cliff path without any nervous rushing but chose a direct passage and jumped each rock precisely, without undue delay, or daydreaming, or adventure-mongering. Glimpsing sideways, I noticed feathered skeletons of unfortunate birds, and the dead sheep, viewed now on our returning route, was in fact half-eaten and eyeless.

The sea line had already crept above the path we'd taken into the gully. Now we'd have to climb higher, where the rock was covered in grass and was perhaps more slippy and certainly less exposed for safe footholds. I smiled. This was even more exciting and more dangerous and I loved the challenge, the thrill of being scared. We'd most definitely return and deliberately wait just twenty minutes longer, to see how we'd escape next time! We'd test the boundary of safety which we'd set ourselves. It was our secret – a child's pledge not to reveal to grown-ups who would relish indulging in adult 'whys and why nots', ladling excess, until all that remained was that final promise, extracted from us, not to return there ever again. A promise which couldn't be broken and which would prevent that lovely feeling of fright bubbling just below our throats – bubbling like a summer ocean of delight!

On storm-grey days with no horizon to separate sea and sky, we would huddle above the cliff face, like sheltering rabbits under a bruised violet sky and observe a violent murderous sea and a forbidden shore. We would not venture down like the yellow wagtail, impishly jumping from the teeth of the waves, teasing the sea to foam. We knew our limitations and paid heed to them. When tart coldness nipped just once more, we'd girlishly go home.

But the sea was still in us, like a drug, or a poison, and we had a craving for more of it. It whipped up our senses and we needed it and we were always greedy for more. It held a bittersweet attraction, which made it special.

9

Change

Christmas, coming as it does in midwinter, brought joyful relief to cold gloomy days which turned into daylight after 9am, but had turned back into night before 3pm. The lack of light was depressing and we bairns sat around the fire drinking each teapot of tea with Mam and Nana until we were in danger of becoming adult! But come the second week of December, Nana would wait until an appropriate weekend and then brought out the cardboard box of decorations.

Now we'd uncoil two-inch-wide rolls of coloured, crinkled crepe paper, changing randomly in the roll from pink/green to blue/orange. They were twisted to their full length and pinned up diagonally on the ceiling, in the corners, with pairs of balloons. Red paper lanterns were hung in the looped spaces in between.

Nana had an artificial tree made of goose feathers, dyed green. On the wire 'branches' we hung brittle glass balls, some with hollowed-out, mother-of-pearl centres, like the insides of sea-shells. At the top of the tree, overseeing all, sat the fairy. She was old with a faded pink crepe paper skirt. She was past her best but she was soon dusted down, because she was as much part of our Christmas as Santa.

No evergreens, such as holly and ivy, were ever brought indoors, as they were considered unlucky: many evil spirits clung desperately under their leaves once the deciduous trees had shed theirs. It would be foolish to bring them indoors to find new hiding places. So they formed no part of a traditional northern Christmas.

Two weekends later Christmas came. I certainly believed Santa

came down a chimney. The morning began with Christmas stockings! We ignored the bitter nip of dampness in the bedroom and rummaged through the stocking, discarding the tangerine and apple in favour of unwrapping gold-foiled chocolate coins and eating these while inspecting the small toys, deeper inside. Santa was always good to us. Then it was downstairs for a hasty breakfast and then finally family presents of slippers, gloves, an annual or storybook, and for me, always dolls.

I loved dolls. I liked their expressions: the way they always seemed on the brink of a chuckle. I liked their thick hair, rooted in narrow furrows across their vinyl heads to reveal no bald patches. It could be combed and washed five times a day and still remain attractive. Mam had knitted dresses, coats, hats, socks, mittens, vests and even pants for them.

Not being a believer in 'you can get too much of a good thing', I asked for twins one Christmas, and that's how I came by Mary and Louise, complete with twin knitted outfits. Mary's hair was not as curly as Louise's, and Mary had a shyer expression but I loved them both identically.

Another Christmas I asked for, but was surprised to receive twin black dolls whom I called Cindy and Lulu. They were smaller than Mary and Louise but their blackness was beautiful. Mam had knitted bright-red party dresses for them. These were flared at the hem and around the neck she had sewn on pearl beads which formed a necklace. The red suited them perfectly and there was some jealousy amongst the other dolls!

Derek received a clockwork, tin train set one year. It chugged round on a figure-of-eight track and was endlessly fascinating.

But I was more envious of the tin police car, battery-operated, which ran along the floor hitting things, reversing and continuing with its siren sounding and patrol light flashing. It was the first battery-driven toy we'd seen and because of that, the batteries must have only lasted a couple of days, if that!

Christmas was a time when children were always indulged with presents. Grown-ups watched, sharing the excitement before starting on the Christmas dinner. The dinner was always three courses with roast chicken, rather than turkey. Usually the hen was given by a neighbour, oven-ready. But once Mam was given an unplucked hen in Thurso. She went to the shed with a perfumed hankie tied round her nose and pulled out enough feathers to stuff a cushion! Since that day she's never been fond of chicken, so quite often we'd have pork or roast beef, instead, for Christmas lunch.

Mam may have been country raised, but despite inbred thriftiness, she enjoyed pretty fancy things. From her teenage years, she followed the fashions of the time and was the first girl in the village to wear trousers. Quite outrageous then!

Nana's sister, who'd emigrated to America, would send back dresses in fine fabrics and Mam, with her slender figure and mass of long black hair, fastidiously pin-curled, must have looked a real stunner. Had it not been for the Second World War, she would never have joined the ATS and never have met Dad, who was likewise stationed in Orkney.

Dad came from Derbyshire with its peaks and dales, babbling brooks and village greens, hustle and bustle, colourful roses and spreading oaks – Orkney must have seemed so desolate to him, so quiet, so flat, so treeless, so ravaged, without the war. After the war and after they were married in Latheron, they spent a few years in Liverpool before coming to live in Caithness. Liverpool had been different, altogether different, large and scary, and not what Mam was used to. There were gangs and killings and she had a young child now and was pregnant again. Now Dad travelled around with his job and was sometimes away overnight. Nights without him were worst. Then there was a murder in a nearby street. Enough was enough. Mam wanted home. Home to somewhere safer, quieter and calmer. Thurso would do. It was big enough. It was a relief to be back in Caithness, back to the same routine.

Children, too, feel secure with routine in their lives: knowing the pattern of tomorrow is important, just like knowing in advance of impending holidays, or knowing on Friday that Saturday in Latheronwheel is just around the corner. To breathe its cool, calm antiseptic air which cleansed a difficult or draining week at school, where learning seemed endless and relevant only to teachers and parents, and a child ended up learning to appease grown-ups, rather than with an excitement, or tingling curiosity, to learn. The actual process of passing tests, when the brain has to sift out relative data, to provide acceptable answers, was in itself quite rewarding – as was the bar of chocolate provided by the teacher and given to a handful of top pupils, on Fridays. And in the early primaries, when school was a prison, that bar of chocolate was my only impetus to learn. Learning gradually, and through an apathy to rebel, became a habit, and as toys became less interesting, then books took over.

Then, when the routine seemed mapped out for years to come; when life was easy and the routine satisfying as a stomach filled, or a grin spreading; when happiness overflowed like trickling rivulets in the burn; when the very air was kissable, Nana moved back to the village, to a new council house.

It was warmer, larger, cosier, with an inside toilet, a proper kitchen, two open fires, garden back and front, and neighbours. An eleven-year-old could see the advantages to an elderly Nana, but inside that eleven-year-old girl, a six-year-old cried for those days and memories of the Lodge, cut surely to the quick that they were gone forever. The Lodge might become a magnificent dream – the detail dripping away as water through a colander, fading even as the eyes open to the reality of morning, and in that split-second when eyes focus, the dream slips away – despite the brain trying desperately to retain it, it only grabs onto parts – while the essence of the dream drifts away downstream to a sea of everyone's lost unconscious dreams and into a darkness that eyes cannot perceive, or take meaning from.

But it wasn't the move to the village, nor the surrendering to learning which shook me out of my childhood of dolls, fairies, witches and daydreams, and weekend days drifting merrily into each other; nor was it the patience of Time to indulge my selfishness, and parents who were just 'there' to comfort and encourage, but not make demands that I should be anything but childish – no, it was when my father died. He was forty-eight, I was twelve.

He had lived only a year after having a stroke. I had known him only as a child knows a father. He was the buckle on the secure belt tied round the family. I had asked nothing of him, just him being on the edge of my consciousness was enough and all that I, the child, had needed. I knew what he liked but had no measure of how much he liked it. As a teenager, I would have sought his advice, asked his opinion and listened while he spoke, for he was an intelligent, sensitive man. But this was not to be. I was still a child and had asked nothing.

I didn't blame myself for that selfishness of a child who was allowed to wander and experience being alone to roam hill and burn and then to return to the warm hug of family, but I did blame myself for believing, childishly, that Dad would get better. I trusted, childishly, in the abilities of doctors to heal. I trusted, childishly, that God would not snatch a 'good' man when the world overflowed with 'bad' men. I trusted, childishly, in the solidity of Family which relied on every member to be there, to be a whole unit.

With these three positive thoughts in my head, I decided that it would just be a few weeks before Dad would recover. 'Weeks' were then amended to months. One evening in Thurso, I was playing outside with Carinda, when a girl whom I didn't know came up to me and said, 'Your Dad's very ill, isn't he? Is he going to die?' Her questions were absurd. How dare she, whom I did not know nor care to know, chat so casually about someone she did not know nor care to know? But her words were already a knife opening a wound of doubt in the pit of my stomach. A wound which was tied up so tightly with positive belief. A wound which couldn't and shouldn't be opened, because Dad wouldn't die, would he?

Dad was a clever, convivial man, an accountant, and great with numbers and games of strategy, like bridge and card games generally. I played draughts with him when he was ill and made stupid moves, knowingly, to let him win. But he would lose interest and struggle for words in that brain that was once lucid and perceptive. His condition worsened and he lay and didn't speak. He just lay there withering in front of our eyes and we could do nothing to help him.

We were not embarrassed by him. We would have kept him and loved him in any state. Though I wish that were really true. I did feel embarrassed and shocked to my soul that I allowed myself to linger and play contentedly with that feeling, for I was thinking of myself, and not of Dad. But the person who lay there was becoming a stranger. Warm summer days with birdsong were annoying and not synchronised with the darkness and depression inside our house. I prayed for Dad to hold on to the long rasping breaths. I prayed for a miracle. Then I woke one morning to an uneasy silence and Mam's face, loaded with emotion, needed no explanation.

He was gone. Mam took us to see him, later, in the coffin in the back room. I wanted to see him. He was still Dad. He looked peaceful and serene. Tension was eased from his face. I felt glad that the pain had at last gone, and he need suffer no more. Later, alone, I went in and kissed him goodbye and I prayed that heaven would be a place where spirits could laugh and talk and have fun and run like children up the Strath, carefree and free from pain.

With death came relief. Relief from all the drama and tension which stained every second of every day, whether Dad was ill at home, or hundreds of miles away in hospital; relief from the feeling that to laugh, even for a moment, was somehow wicked and uncaring; relief that the wondering 'when' and 'if' was over.

However, that relief was to be a mere, small sweetish gasp of respite, something tiny and soon insignificant, as I began to realise that Dad was gone forever. I'd never see him again, or talk to him, or notice him grow older. I'd never know if he would be proud of me, or if I'd have made him happy. Mine was a selfish grief. I wondered how I'd manage without a father; the experiences I'd miss out on, the embarrassing awkwardness of friends towards me. I suppose I'd hoped that we'd all pull together, Mam, Margaret and me with the help of Nana and Derek, so that we could still be a family, like we were at weekends. But I'd reckoned without Mam's grief.

It was deep and prolonged. An adult grief which I did not understand and which lingered long after the constant callers, long after the funeral, long after the curtains were opened and long after the persistent odour of chrysanthemums. A grief which she held close to herself like a warm comfortable shawl. For that was all she had left, Grief, and now the responsibility of bringing up two children, alone. All the effort, freely given, of doing everything for Dad, month after long month, and being found inadequate as she saw it, gave way to a private despair which we could not get close to, to help. Her sorrow was long-lasting and deeply etched and I often feared it would engulf her – and if I lost her, I would be truly desolate. Very, very gradually her strength of spirit returned and she became Mam again, more sensitive, more easily upset, more protective, but more maternal.

There was no routine, nothing dependable, nothing predictable, only chaos. I was cocooned in grief. It held me tight, warmly swaddled like the baby I was turning back into. It was comforting but unnatural. I was suffocating. I needed to break free. I now stood on the bottom of a deep dark pit of gloom. I latched onto any slender means of escape. At best, it would be a lifeline. At worst, I would just fall back to the bottom again. I couldn't fall any further, though. I plucked up courage and asked Mam if we could have a puppy, a Jack Russell puppy.

Some years previously, while we had been visiting Dad's sisters in Derbyshire, we had been sitting on a bank of the River Dove, relaxing after climbing Thorpe Cloud, when we were amused by the antics of a small, cheeky Jack Russell terrier. We had never seen one before in Caithness and even Mam had commented on the pup. He had seemed an ideal dog and all in such a neatly-sized package. Why Mam did not disagree to the idea of us having a dog after Dad died, I cannot answer. But I persistently followed up any adverts in the local paper whenever Jack Russells were mentioned for sale.

Eventually I received a letter from a contact in Wigan, saying she had a Jack Russell-cross-Corgi pup for sale. Her writing was scrawly and where I'd read, 'He's a right terrier', I was, days after owning him, to discover she had actually written, 'He's a right terror'.

After arrangements were made and he was duly paid for, we all went up to Thurso Railway Station, where we were handed a slatted wooden crate with a tiny shivering form inside.

His journey had been long, perhaps as long as ten hours, and we were unsure if he had been given any food or water in all that time. No soul, grieving or otherwise, could fail to be moved to pity. Many a pup would not have survived such a journey. But this was no ordinary pup, for he had an unwritten task: to bring distraction, relief, hope, brightness, fun, caring and love back into the lives of a family in turmoil. He was more than adequate for the job and no pet was as important in my life as he was.

He was our lifeline out of that pit of gloom. In no conceivable way could he replace Dad, but he was something to receive all that love which would have been freely given to Dad, if only he had lived. I would have promised anything to have Dad back, but I wasn't given the choice. What was done, was done. Dad was snatched away from me too soon and I had years of love still waiting in reserve, banked up over years of childhood, to be spent on him later. But it was not to be. The pressure of not being able to use it up was overwhelming and needed release. In this respect, the pup was perfect.

10

Kim

Once home, Mam opened the wooden orange box. Out jumped a sandy-coloured puppy wagging his docked tail furiously with relief and excitement. Cowering behind the couch, or anxiously sniffing, slowly and stealthily, round the corners of his new home were not the characteristics of this pup. Cautious restraint was never one of his attributes. He tore round the flat on power-surged legs, barking and snarling. The more we ran, the more he ran. He grabbed and clung on by his incisors to our skirts. At that moment, I stood up on the front corner of the bath to escape his crazed lunging. We'd bought a pinball puppy! Eventually, he wore off the coiled-up energy restrained by the hours of confinement in the train and he accepted food and water.

At last, we had a chance to look at him properly. His head and features were Jack Russell but his ginger colouring was Corgi. He had a white chest and four white ankle socks. Between his front feet and his back feet, his body moved continuously, concertina-like. This dog had 'mischief' written through him like a stick of rock.

Mam said he'd need a short name, so that he would always recognise it, and when one of us suggested 'Kim' out loud, he seemed to turn round in response. So we called him 'Kim', not realising then that it would be a name we'd always be shouting in quadruplicate. Perhaps he grew to dislike his name, perhaps he never knew it was his name, for he rarely answered to it! But that was when he grew up and became human with a mind of his own.

But now he was just a wriggly pup who loved attention. He

peeped and whimpered in his box in the hall that first night, then sniffed and snorted and pawed at our bedroom door. 'Okay. Let him in. Just tonight,' Mam said with determination. 'He's had an awful journey and he must be lonely, poor thing.'

From that night he always slept on, or more truthfully in, Margaret's bed or mine. I woke one morning and saw his head sharing my pillow, with his little body under the covers. He looked, for the life of him, like a brown teddy bear. Mam was horrified and Kim soon learned that he should sleep on top of the quilt at the bottom of the bed – at least until she turned the light out. I suppose we ruined any chance of him remaining doggy.

In no time, we taught him to beg, give-a-paw, fetch, lie, sit and stay, and how to retrieve things in the bath which were attached to the end of a long string, by means of a two-paw hauling-in method. All these tricks he perfected in return for chocolate drops – his enthusiasm waning as the box of rewards emptied. (I, too, had known about the persuasive power of chocolate when it came to learning.) But he taught himself other tricks like defurring the lining of one of Mam's best, suede winter boots, shaking it with the ferocity of a working Jack Russell terrier.

And who was it that sneaked quietly behind the couch at Nana's with the soup bone, which had been soaking in a pan of water on the kitchen table? And who was the thief who pinched raw mince from Mam's shopping bag and defied us with bared teeth to retrieve it, then slept soundly, bloated with happiness, while we ate cheese sandwiches?

The catalogue of his misdemeanours was long and grave. For instance, if I stopped in the street to chat to friends, I would feel my leg warming and sure enough, he'd piddled on my trouser leg. This had the desired effect of cutting short my conversation and returning us hurriedly home. Was it planned as such? His attitude was arrogant and stubborn, but Kim was the pet I'd always been looking for: a pet who responded to touch and sensed when I was morose and dispirited. Then he would poke

his muzzle under my elbow, making it flap against his nose until I was forced to stroke him. Or else, he became a jester and entertained us by circling faster and faster trying to catch his docked tail, like a canine spinning top. There is nothing like laughter to dissipate a bout of self-pity and anxiety.

Life, too, was gaining impetus. Mam went out to work and so did Margaret. Margaret also took driving lessons so that she could drive us to Latheronwheel. Dad was not being replaced, rather these changes were made out of necessity, for survival, to re-implement a routine.

At weekends, when Margaret drove us along the Causeway Mire to Nana's, Kim would keep his nose close to the air vent, sniffing for a hint of saltiness in the air, and listening out for the click-click-clicking of the right-hand indicator and with that, the inevitability that Latheronwheel was just three minutes away. Then he would squeak with joy and dance backwards and forwards on Mam's knee until her tights were stippled in holes from his sharp claws and she'd elbow him back saying something like, 'Aye, aye, we're here'.

He had a taste for life which was childlike – indeed, he was hyperactive! He bounced through long grass like a rubber ball, for he wanted to see everything and not be restricted by obvious obstacles.

He would not accept that grass, twelve inches above his head, was an obstacle. Every few sniffs of grass were logged 'worthy of more intensive investigation' for another day. We again observed Nature at a running pace. Creatures were flushed out of the undergrowth in fear, and now we viewed animals in flight, rather than feeding, as we had done in the pre-puppy days. That dog crashed and yapped his way through the wood like a brash boy-adventurer. Every bird which at the last unsafe second was squawked into flight, was followed two feet into the air. Accompanying the inevitable thud of him landing in a heap on the ground was a look of sheer incomprehension as to what he'd done wrong because then, and for many years to come, he always believed he would be able to fly – if only he could figure out the right method of take off.

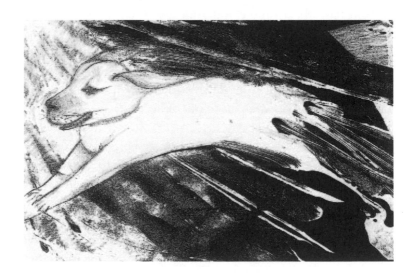

He may have been small in stature but he was big on ambition. At the Shore, I could throw him a ball-sized stone, one which his soft mouth could clasp effortlessly, but he would deliberately sniff out a huge boulder which would stick out of both corners of his mouth. This was the only one he would insist on carrying up the braehead and all the way back to Nana's. His head could be bent at any awkward angle, but jaw down, he would girn and complain on and up the hill. Every so often he'd stop to rearrange his stone-swollen mouth. But home he would take it, drop it heavily on the doorstep and saunter past Nana, tail up, eyes shining, with a grin the size of Asia.

Now that Nana lived in the village, there were neighbours with cats to bark at and hens to chase. The stray grains of an idea of a chase may have just rolled about emptily in his brain, but once they joined together, they swelled and thickened quickly, came rapidly to the boil and formed a notion which would be irresistible. For instance, there was the incident with Cissy's hens.

Cissy had a cottage just across the road from Nana's and at right angles to it. From Nana's doorstep, a dog was presented with an uninterrupted view of the henhouse at the bottom of the flagstone path which led past Cissy's front door. One day, Cissy's hens were idly gossiping, heads bobbing, chins wagging, in her garden while Kim, the pup, sat on Nana's doorstep gazing nonchalantly seawards towards a distant horizon taking in the view like a cloth-capped fisherman chewing tobacco. Gradually Kim's body took on a right-to-left, left-to-right motion as his head seesawed from side to side in time to the hens' higher-pitched 'reallys'. He still stared at the ocean but his nose began to twitch ever so slightly. I had come to recognise that I had roughly five seconds before he would bound off, introduce himself and add another element to the conversation.

I leant forward slowly, speaking gently, to grab his collar but he was already off without ever looking at me. I had faded into the background like the horizon. He didn't hear me shout. He had forgotten his name. He had forgotten about the crate, his terrible journey, how I'd covered for him when he'd piddled on the living-room carpet, how I'd fed him those chocolate biscuits secretly. He had forgotten it all. His concentration was canine, rigid and unswervable.

He leapt the garden gate beautifully like a champion and went straight down Cissy's path, completely unembarrassed. I gave chase, desperately embarrassed, and hoped that Cissy was out, or at least in a back room. Next I heard the loud shrieks of hens as they scattered onto walls, through the midden and flew squawking onto shed roofs – feathers dropping like litter from a schoolboy's pocket. When I eventually caught him, his eyes shone with wicked pleasure and a shameless grin filled his face. I scolded him severely, explained at length why he shouldn't chase hens, and he looked straight into my eyes and licked my hands. He seemed to understand. There was something in his cloying sweetness that I wanted to trust.

However, en route to the Shore one weekend, Kim deliberately mismatched our pace and sidled slowly, nose down, on the pretence of tracking the stain of something suspicious, alongside Jimmy's cottage. Kim was just at the gate when both Margaret and I whistled on him to come, but he nipped in through the open gate and into the back garden. In a scurry and a screeching about four or five bantam hens flew onto the cottage roof, while the cockerel flew raucously above us towards the wood. This trick accomplished, Kim tore after us and walked innocently to heel until we rounded the corner, on and out of sight, to the Shore. All three of us then sniggered.

From further down the hill, we couldn't hear Jimmy so clearly shouting, 'My poor cockie. Where's my poor cockie?' Until then, I'd believed hens to be flightless. We never found out if the bantam cock returned. We didn't dare ask. After that Kim was kept on a lead until we passed every house in the village.

Although Kim couldn't fly, he could jump. He leapt ditches, gates and fences with ease. Although agile and nippy, he never caught anything – except one rabbit stupid with myxomatosis.

But it wasn't through lack of trying. And he could dig. He would burrow holes to command. If Nana had a hedge to transplant, he'd be in there, risking decapitation from her spade, with his front feet furiously tunnelling like a mechanical miniature excavator. Roots were then pulled out like bootlaces.

He was always in the midst of everything. When Nana made up the fire, Kim pinched coal and gnawed it behind the couch. If he was cold, he would simply lie on the tiled fireplace until the frying heat sent him first onto the rug, and then, eventually, he would throw himself carelessly against the living-room door with a noisy collapsing of bones and a deep bored sighing. He chose the door to sleep against so that no-one could leave without him knowing. But if he crept onto a chair, curled so comfortably that no-one had the heart to move him, then he would sleep content-edly for hours with his eyebrows twitching and his paws tapping out a morse code of indecipherable doggy adventures. Any noise at all might wake him and he'd toss everyone a look which seemed to ask, 'What next?' He had a low boredom threshold.

This trait was useful when we visited relatives, because when it got close to four o'clock, and eventually perfected to three minutes either side of 4pm, Kim would rise from the fireside and sweep us a look. If no-one got up to leave, he would always approach Nana, lick her hand and then proceed to beg and squeak continuously in front of her. He pleaded persistently with Nana to go home, drowning out and then halting all conversation. All eyes were on this circus dog with his self-taught act. Nana would smile. But she got up and said, 'Well, the dowg's telling us it's time to go home.' When Nana rose, we all could. That dog could achieve something that I would be too embarrassed to suggest and in such a light-hearted way, a childish cheek that no-one could take offence at.

He was afraid of nothing, despite being a small dog. He approached wolfhounds and snarling Alsatians on Thurso Beach with a view to fight. He was a hunter and he was fearless. He was a young Derek in the wood. He had spirit. I learned much from that dog. If I gave him childish attributes, it was because I felt my childhood was over and I had to come to terms with Dad's dying in an adult way. I felt it was wrong to remember rushing shrieking times, gushing with happiness, that they must be gone. Time had allowed me to be golden and I had flown with fairies and fought with invisible demons, but I was no Wendy and there was no Neverland. I was not the princess I had imagined myself to be a few years earlier. I did not lord it over Latheronwheel and there was no guarantee of 'happily ever after'. A chill wind had closed the nursery door. It wouldn't open again.

I stood in the dark anteroom of adulthood, stripped of clues, all my lucky wishes used up. My time was up. The game was over. I had tasted adulthood – its grief, its sorrow, its black worry and its grey future – and I didn't like it. I liked neither its responsibilities, nor its compromise. It was unfair and many an adult arm could have cuddled me with a soft flabby warmness and pitied me and cooed, 'Poor wee thing.' I could have wallowed in that feeling of unfairness for years and no-one would have minded. A thick red pen-line had been drawn through my life between childhood and adulthood. It was too sudden. I had passed 'Go' without knowing the rules.

But then there was Kim. His nipping zest for life was acid and sparkling and childlike. He saw life as I'd once seen it: a tingling curiosity of all the senses, a radiating glow of thankfulness for being born – that chance of life, so primitive, so simple, so precious. Now, when I was sad, he was happy; when I was cold, he was warm; when I was afraid, he was fearless. He was a little bundle of joy which I had in my corner. He was my secret weapon, my ally against fast-encroaching adulthood. He taught me how to laugh again without feeling ashamed to be happy, and so smoothed out the edges of that dark line between childhood and adulthood. He stitched that wound which had opened and had threatened to let in a dark morbid infection.

After a bad day at school, I would return home to a welcome of pure gladness unrestrained and unvaried, unrestricted by how I looked or how I felt, not dependent on first exchanging pleasantries or quips or asking forgiveness for past misdemeanours, nothing mattered. It was an undiluted welcome which only dogs can repeatedly give. A welcome which is dependable and reliable. It was special and medicinal. It was the tonic I needed.

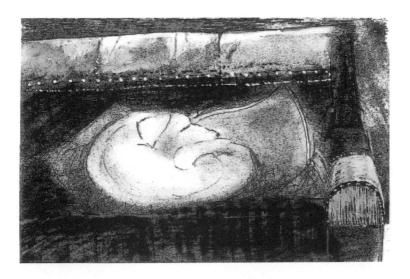

11

Red, Black, White and Grey

Walking around Latheronwheel with Margaret, or Derek when he wasn't loudly showing off and demanding all my attention, was also a measure of refreshing summer-fruit cordial – it was sweetly pleasurable. In the village there were other girls of my age whom I could have befriended and played with. Thankfully I had been called shy, and this suited my purposes perfectly because I didn't want a 'friend' who would prattle on, having decided that the escape from adult company was an opportunity to chat noisily and constantly about nothing in particular. At least Margaret and I knew when to keep the same silences. Another 'friend', interested only in her own loudness, would have made our walk purposeless and useless – for, in front of receptive eyes was an open chocolate box of adventures. And Margaret and I would dip into an adventure and select something sweet or crunchy, as randomly as the scenes Nature presented to us. Everything, however small, was delicious and we shared it together.

Having other friends, therefore, was not always companionable, and conversely, being alone was not always lonely. Up the Strath, I could happily sit alone, stuck solid like granite, fossilstill, on top of an age-old stone and feel the wind strengthening in roaring gusts through the bent old birch trees as I listened for buzzards and looked for adders; or at the Shore I could clamber down a rocky shelf, pick a path along the sealine, huddle cosily alone under a hard sharp overhang and observe the vastness of ocean with a pack of waves running through a mauve middle distance; or I could walk through the Shore Park by the cliffs as far as Knockinnon, alone, with no human within a half-mile radius – totally alone – I could lie down in the short grass amongst tiny trefoils, under an immense spread of infinite sky, dotted and dashed with gulls.

Nature was a special friend and dependable. Her temperament was predictable through each season. That there might be a hailstorm in June or a heatwave in March only increased her variety and charm. However, friendship is infinite and fallible and sometimes there is a need to sample something new and unknown and spicy. Or sometimes circumstances change. People change. Places change.

Latheronwheel had certainly changed. A broad new road was built which sliced through the wood and cut the village in half. Since the building of the atomic reactor at Dounreay in the '50s, Caithness had become a busy place. Many locals found well-paid jobs there, and more workers came from the south to supervise the unskilled workforce. All this led to more people and more traffic. Old bridges, like the one near the Strath, could no longer support the weight of lorries now going over it and besides, the main road between the Lodge and the village was narrow and twisty with tight corners for lorries to negotiate.

So a new road was blasted out of the wood. When finished it flew past the top of the village, the shops, the Hotel and the signpost to the Shore. Sightseers whizzed past the Whale Bone Gate and didn't stop any more to take photographs. No-one even noticed the pile of rubbish opposite – once the Lodge. The village school had long since closed, the churches were under-used, the manse was empty and villagers drove to Wick for cheaper shopping. Robert-the-shoemaker became Robert-the-post. Derek got a job at the Gamekeeper's. When the Palmers came north in August, Derek took six gun dogs, three straining brutes leashed to each hand, to the hill for the pheasant shoot. It was honest work but tough. I visited him once. Amongst the frenzied yapping and loud yelping, Derek was stirring something in an oil drum with a stick. It smelt a putrid brew. Smirking, he opened the lid to reveal boiling sheep's heads, their eyeballs floating in the watery stinky stock.

And bits and pieces of my childhood bobbed around me here and there – ripped way from the whole in chunks, chopped up and stewed. Everything changed as surely as the unused old road by the bridge narrowed, as its sides gathered first with soil and then with grass and weeds and moss. And, in such a short time, it became hard to believe that traffic had ever passed there and easier to believe that maybe I had imagined everything. Cars, buses and lorries roared past in the distance on that new broad road straight out of Latheronwheel.

Everything speeded up. I held my childhood in my hands like a winter snowball, but the more I clasped it, the faster it melted in my warm hands and dripped away. I had to lay it down and get on with my life. I couldn't dwell on 'what was', or 'what could have been'. I had to concentrate on 'now'. Now I was a teenager. I was growing and changing. I had to gather up most of the bits of 'shyness', squeeze them into a plasticine ball and mould them into something else, something more acceptable. I had to change. I had to compress all the sights and smells of childhood into an essence of Strathness, pour it into an empty aspirin bottle, put on the lid and hide it under my pillow.

No-one would befriend a shy girl who preferred to rush away on a magic carpet of thought, instead of idly gossiping. And I longed to be with girls who giggled in groups, like newly-fed starlings, in the school cloakroom on Monday mornings. I envied the pairs of boys and girls, preened and beautiful, who walked to school so close and sat in the cloakroom, wrapped round each other, so close, covered in a warm scarf of love. Nobody wanted to know about solitude, birdsong, shrill winds, sea waves and infinity. All they talked about was boys and bands and dancing with boys and togetherness and 'now' and boys.

I liked the taste of this. This was different and spicy. This was a new assortment. I could become like them, gregarious even. I could clip on a mask and act differently. I could pull on different clothes and look different. I could look like them. I would become less green, and hopefully less red!

I'd redden when a friend paid me a compliment, with which I wholeheartedly agreed, but felt it only right to disagree with. I blushed when I just meant to titter at vulgar jokes. I blushed when anyone asked, 'What do you think of that then?' It might have been a boring explanation of an event about which my support was needed and my undivided attention was expected, but over which I had sprayed a heady scent of Strathness. And I was somewhere else, somewhere secret, lost, backward, stammering, 'umming' and 'welling' for time to think of something general and acceptable, while my pink face was already darkening to scarlet.

I could take a deep breath and prevent myself from crying on occasions but I could never stop myself from blushing. Anyone could say to me, 'You're blushing', even when I wasn't, but just after they'd said it and I'd heard it, I would redden out of control. Who needed rouge to enhance cheekbones? Mine seemed perpetually naturally red.

My legs, on the other hand, were unnaturally tanned with nylon stockings, for I had discovered from Carinda that she wore them under her white knee socks, not for extra warmth but as a fashion statement. Then I would have to be the same. I found an old suspender belt of Mam's at the back of a drawer in her bedroom. I went to Woolworths and bought a pair of nylons size 8, in 'American Tan'.

Because I was still skinny, and Mam's suspender elastic had stretched, the belt hung halfway down my hips before it fastened securely. Nevertheless, I hooked up my stockings and pulled up my socks. Yes, they looked okay. I was slightly worried that the stocking tops hung so low that the broad band of white 'untanned' skin above them might show. It didn't strike me as odd that I would be pale faced and white-armed but amazingly American tanned-legged!

Of course, seamed stockings completely gave the game away, so I had to scan the packets of stockings for 'seamless' ones. I finally settled on size 9, which wrinkled annoyingly above the elastic of my knee socks, but were at least longer. Even as I unwrapped them and held them in each hand to dangle as flat brown-paper legs, I could see that the shape of size 9 legs were more curvaceous than mine. Still, Mam bought me my own suspenders, which tied at my waist, and someone somewhere was inventing tights which would cling to the narrowest of twig-legs.

When I was younger I wore anything to keep warm. Now, I could only wear clothes which I liked the look of, or rather, ones similar to friends' and which looked good on them – but perhaps not so good on me? No matter which configuration of triptych dressing-table mirrors reflected in varied acute angles of a held-open wardrobe-door mirror I set up in the bedroom, I couldn't properly see how I looked from behind. Although I could achieve perhaps a 90% overall view, it would be that 10% hidden view which I would irrationally worry about.

Many a Saturday morning I would stand in front of the

mirrors in different outfits, agonising over which one I should wear to go up the busy High Street. Which one? What if I met a boy I liked? What would he think if he saw me in something horrible? Strangely, it didn't bother me at all, what he might be wearing. If I couldn't decide, I would just stay in. It was as silly and important as that.

My clothes hung on my skinny frame of a body. When I was a youngster, Mam had bought me a kilt in the Forbes tartan. She said the kilt would give me more bulk – it was certainly weighty! I wore it one Sunday up the Strath, where we'd gone on a family walk. I was jumping between some stones in the burn when next I was up to my waist in water with my kilt floating around me like a huge, green-checked, tropical water lily. Laughing, Mam pulled me out of the cold water and, as soon as I emerged, each pleat clung round my knees and I became a red sea anemone above the tide-line.

I could smile about it now, as a teenager, looking back. Childhood had been so easy, so much fun. My body was now running into adolescence with swallow-speed. Chemicals were coursing through it, changing it surely as a caterpillar changes into a butterfly. Yet I never felt certain that I would pupate and reach the beautiful butterfly stage. All I knew for sure was that I had become an all-over smelly, hairy spotty grub.

I searched through all Mam's magazines for information about womanhood. I read all about puberty, periods, divorce, adultery and the 'change-of-life'. There was a lot to take in. How I wished I could have a bust to be proud of. Nothing seemed to be happening under my vest. Perhaps I would remain boobless. More and more girls in my class were wearing bras with snooty arrogance.

It was with relief that I discovered that some enlarging busts were unnatural. Like the girl who stuffed her bikini top with paper hankies to a firm B cup, before diving into the swimming pool with the rest of her classmates. A few minutes later the implants floated soggily to the surface and remained around her

like the flowers around the drowned Ophelia in that pre-Raphaelite painting. I bet she wished she was dead. No-one believed her when she declared that she had a heavy cold and had to keep the tissues somewhere! Her embarrassment was my embarrassment, for I felt sure that I might have done the same thing, if only I had thought of it first.

My long hair, which in my primary days had been neatly tied at the top of my head with a ribbon, was now parted in the middle with a thick fringe cut just above my eyebrows, and was left loose. In class, when I was bent over my school books, It hung forward like spaniel's ears and concealed the odd spot and cheeks on the verge of a blush. I twiddled and mouthed strands of it often and unconsciously.

I'm not sure why I asked Carinda's sister, a hairdresser, to cut it. I had never had it short before. After it was cut and everyone said it suited me, I rushed home and set up the mirrors. Mam

said it suited me, Margaret likewise, but I cried. It was both short
and revealing. I could no longer disguise my feelings behind a
curtain of hair. Every nuance of emotion, every twitch of temper,
every fleeting but terrible mood, every needle-pricking slight,
every blush and every spot were now on view from all angles. I
was too old to hide behind a cardboard Hallowe'en mask. I was
too old for make-believe. The bright light of childhood was
dulling. A new me was being pushed under the spotlight to take
centre-stage.

But I hadn't yet become vivacious and gaudy-bright. I wasn't
that confident. I hadn't reached that stage of development. I was
more like those small green caterpillars which dangle from
silken threads and rotate like dizzy puppets from trees in late
summer. To me, Mam was my tree – solid, strong and supportive
throughout childhood. She had been my centre – the person I
most wanted to impress and love. However, I didn't want her
now to pull my strings. I would do things my way, without her
parental advice and common sense and attitudes (but please
don't drop me). I would deliberately annoy her and shock her
and hurt her feelings (but please don't cut the string). She alone
would be privy to a gamut of powerful emotion, untempered,
running wild without tact or remorse, unstoppable like a
turning wave (but please still love me).

Friends, on the other hand, only saw a pleasant me, smiling
and witty, fashionable and fun, for this was the me I had
practised in front of mirrors, the likeable me, the me I had
groomed and was proud of. The other me lurked around in dark
corners of my mind. She was so ferocious and I loathed her so
much that I preferred to keep her hidden. Perhaps I was a
changeling – a fairy child, or a body taken over by aliens,
because I didn't always recognise myself. And it was so hard to
say 'sorry' to Mam and all that, and besides it was my friends
whom I now wanted to impress.

So if friends wore their mini skirts short, then mine would be
shorter. Tights must have been invented by now because it was

the 'swinging sixties' and no self-respecting teenager wore her skirts more than three inches below her bum, even in winter. Mam moaned at my hemline – little knowing that as soon as I left the house and rounded the corner, I turned the waistband of my skirt round on itself, which had the effect of hitching my skirt an inch or two shorter. I remember male teachers noticing these hemlines, but not immediately complaining. It was flirty and fun! It was a uniform that teachers and parents could not copy and retain their dignity. It was a poke in the eye at authority, and a giggle shared.

After school I returned home and took off this uniform and replaced it with another – denim flares, the wider the better. Pulling on my Melton cloth blazer, I'd head off to the beach or along the cliffs by Victoria Walk, in any weather, with Kim. Being unnaturally gregarious was hard work, and to be alone with Kim was a welcome release from the burden of it all. Besides, walking the dog enabled me to escape the scrutiny of grown-ups – for I always imagined I was being spied on – who would then probably remark, 'Oh there's her out with the dog again' instead of 'What's she doing out on her own? What does she look like? High heels, short skirt . . . if she bent down . . . ' Followed by the afterthought, 'And fancy going out in this weather without a hat'.

Teenagers just did not wear hats, not in any weather. Hoods were even worse. Who wore a hood? Middle-aged women or children under eight maybe, but never teenagers. On the wettest of days, when clouds opened up like water bombs and scored direct hits, we teenagers would saunter home, acting cool, our hair plastered on our skulls like brown swimming caps, leaving ears sticking out enough to give some an ear-complex. Home we'd dawdle, in dribs and drabs, never altering our pace. We'd step off pavements into the paths of cars, never looking sideways, except to intercede with a witty remark to that ragged bunch of friends which dwindled as each one's home got closer; and out of sight we ran indoors to get into the warmness and groaned as mothers mentioned hoods.

Still no-one wore a hood or, God forbid, a rainmate. The latter was a sort of fold-away plastic bag which tied under the chin with tapes – seventy-year-old women wore them because they were handy and lightweight, and middle-aged women popped them on, just after a perm, just in case. I'm sure all our mothers had sneaked one in each of our pockets for a rainy day, but they remained there, untouched, as a secret embarrassment.

We all looked the same. This was necessary in this transition between adolescent and adult. We formed a group of similar-looking youths. We might within our peer group have had different friends and have been part of different cliques, but an older onlooker would not have been able to discern this, as we all looked alike. In this pack we felt no fear. Nothing could touch us. We fed each other on our own opinions and we grew and flourished and became buoyant and floated on a wave of self-confidence, and snapped like seadogs at anyone who thought differently. We needed no adult advice or adult hindsight. Parents were ancient. Forty was ancient. The James Dean in all of us sniggered and gloated, 'If we ever reach that age!' For this was our time, to live by our rules and not someone else's, someone older's, to manipulate and plan for us and re-run as their second chance to be young again. Besides, we were flower children. We would turn into beautiful people.

Flower Power had arrived and at last reached Thurso. Shops full of teenage clothes were now called 'boutiques', and played pop music while we scanned the price labels for something affordably outrageous. Luckily some styles could be copied. With a needle and some embroidery thread, many a plain midi skirt could be embellished with psychedelic daisies in simple stem stitch. Even Derek embroidered and appliquéd both legs of his jeans into a work of art to be proud of.

Even *The People's Friend* – frankly an older person's journal and not on a par with *Jackie* – became an unusual source of fashion items. For instance, when long scarves, one end of which started at the front at hem-length then wound once round the neck and ended up at the back hem-length, became high fashion, I sent off to The People's Friend for two identical mohair scarves. When they arrived, Mam wove the ends together to form an invisible join and, hey-presto, I had a boa constrictor of a scarf to be proud of! It was the subject of many unanswered inquiries.

Psychedelia arrived with a hotchpotch of fluorescent greens, oranges and shocking pinks. There were embroidered cheese-cloth tops and patterned smock dresses with large kipper ties, long ankle-length patchwork dresses, hot pants, crochet waist-coats, stripy tank tops, ponchos, floppy hats, beads, black and white plastic earrings and belts, false eyelashes and stick-on flower transfers.

I watched the Beatles on tv and next day everyone was talking about them. I joined their fan club, and Frank Ifield's, and bought all their records, while Derek bought ones by the Rolling Stones and Pink Floyd. My friends and I knew all the words to all the Beatles' songs and sang along to their records. They had a crush on Paul, but I preferred George. Everything was fab and groovy and every girl wanted to look like Twiggy – a tall skinny waif with dark eyes, white-pink lipstick and cropped hair.

I still had to go to Latheronwheel at weekends while other girls went to discos to get off with older boys. Boys of our own age were still skinny and stunted, dreamt of being football players and never about girls, and still looked up words like 'arse' and 'penis' in the dictionary, for laughs. Older boys, on the other hand, were tall and confident, dark and handsome. So boys, who had been just a few years earlier so endlessly stupid, grotty and irritating, loudly pushing and kicking their way through primary, now became the subject of all daydreams and all conversation. And that 'tingling of the senses' which I had experienced as a child observing nature was now focused on boys.

A boy, whom I had fancied and about whom I had woven the most intricate invention of him-and-me and me-and-him, did not necessarily have to ask my opinion on anything, nor say 'Hello,' but merely had to smile near me or look in my general

direction, to turn my knees to jelly! The sum total of all that I'd been, all that I'd done, all that I had experienced and noted and reflected on, had resulted in me turning into an idiot. And if he spoke to me, I could babble on, blethering about anything he wanted to talk about with false conviction, for I only wanted to hold his attention for about five minutes and cared little about the content of our conversation. Just five minutes and I'd be madly in love!

Being in love is a childish self-indulgent joy. It looks for no faults and therefore finds none. It is blinkered from reason and real life. It bubbles. It is a frenzy of the senses which precludes sense and reasonableness and family advice. It is a 'now' feeling and in that it is childlike – adults live in the past or the future, but never content themselves with now. Being in love is wanting 'now' to be endless and boundless. But 'to never have been so happy' is sometimes wickedly balanced with 'to never have felt so sad' when first love turns sour and walks away without a backward glance. First love is the best love only because it is superficial.

Being an older adolescent is about having personal values and dreams. Sometimes I could be enormously funny and be at the centre of a buzz of attention, or else I could want to be completely alone and retreat selfishly into myself for hours. Both made me equally happy at specific times. Should I be a hedonistic flirt or a philosophical recluse? I liked both and neither. If only I could compromise.

But things are purer black or white, never grey. Greyness is adult – a betrayal of ideals. Being two different people made life complicated and finding a proper boyfriend difficult. When I was with a quiet, T-shirted sensitive boy, I longed to be with a brash, smart, loudmouthed flirt! There were probably boys who were a bit of both, but the compromise would be a dilution of both types: a grey boy, a dull copy, a parody of both. Compromising is the beginning of adulthood. It is lack lustre and flat with no muscle and no fight but is the basis of an adult relationship. I would learn to accept this later, much later.

All the analysing of others and self was tiring to mind and body, so I'd take myself off to my room. After I'd labelled everything into neat piles of Black and White, I'd pack them into their boxes and put them under my bed. Then I'd shut the bedroom door to be privately lethargic and sluggish. I'd stuff my face with chocolate, lie down bloated, and wish for metamorphosis. Surely it wouldn't be long before I would escape my plainness, turn into an articulate bright thing and flit off on a warm air current to a beautiful place, full of beautiful people?

12

Green

I had not pupated but had merely peeled off another layer of outgrown green skin. Yet again my life had changed. It now became me, my friends, Thurso, learning and me. Mam, Margaret, Nana and Derek were being stacked in a pile with Latheronwheel. Although I still walked through Latheronwheel with Margaret and Kim, now it was for exercise, to burn off calories.

There was no running downhill and shrieking about. We might jump thistles for the hell of it, but it was effortfully, mechanically and clownishly with no natural childish rhythm, and afterwards I always checked in case someone had seen me and laughed. There was no pricking sharpness to my vision, either, for I was usually deep in thought about something completely different, something weighty and immense, unrelated to Latheronwheel both in importance and size, and unrelated to Nature and the cycle of life. My eyes were glazed. I saw nothing. Life was serious and Latheronwheel held no mystery now. I had gorged myself on that chocolate box of adventures and I was sick of it. Now it looked plain, ordinary, common and I was educated.

I had never been the cleverest pupil in my class but I had always been amongst them. Oh, I had tried to be top in certain subjects. I wanted to be the best – or what had been the point in learning? However, I reached a stage when I had to accept that no amount of revision, or extra study, would place me ahead of six or seven friends who were consistently bright in every subject, brighter than me, and effortlessly so.

But I had moments of brilliance, when a teacher had selected me for special praise, and I shone out and became golden again.

The event was richly pleasurable. So I sparkled in snatches, as the sun peeping out from behind clouds on an overcast summer day short and fleeting but piercing for that moment. I fed on that warmth and stored it up and craved more of it. Learning took me over and I couldn't get enough of it. It had become an obsession.

Education had promised to open the door to a life unexplored by my parents and would lead to prospects, a career, money and happily-ever-after, in short, a path out of plainness. It was a chance to escape forever from that shrunken green casing which squeezed me tight. I wanted to break free and flutter and flit on that warm air of expectation and be as a gaudy dazzling thing.

Soon enough I was sitting on the train out of Caithness, university-bound, with like-minded, like-humoured, like-dressed classmates, liking each other. En masse we were untouchable. The first five hours to Inverness flew past. Before we knew it we were looking for our connections south. However, the last three hours to Aberdeen dragged by – conversation was sporadic and we all checked our watches, often and nervously. Eventually the long caterpillar train of students chugged slowly and lazily into Aberdeen.

The final leg of our trip had been long and boring with ample time to pupate, to shed that final skin of family and childhood haunts. At Aberdeen Station we threw open the doors, shed our past as final, old dry skins, stepped out of them, smelt the warm

city air, looked forwards and emerged as bright-eyed, sparkling-golden specks of fragile expectation. I waited momentarily for the blood to pump into my wings so that I could fly off on a new adventure, the most important one: the fulfilment of self.

Laughing redcoats breezed amongst us and welcomed us, and sent us to taxis waiting to take us to our Halls of Residence. Out of the station the traffic jarred in constant sharp bursts and the atmosphere was grey and mucky with fumes. The buildings were taller than what I was used to – tightly crammed together to hide the sun. The grey granite looked rough and tough. On the pavements queues of people with bland-grey expressions, drained of laughter, were all urgently going somewhere to do something, imminently. If I stood out there, motionless on the pavement, I would have been brushed aside and stamped on and then overrun by a steady stream of moving maggots. So this was the place I'd spent so long dreaming about. This was Happily-ever-after?

Once at the Halls, I was shown to a small, bare-walled, grey-painted room, complete with bed, desk, chair and wardrobe. Many similar rooms were stacked above each other to form towers where similar students of similar ability and dissimilar childhoods were flung together, imprisoned, to become friends out of necessity in this home from home. Here I sat petless, orphaned, alone. What if teachers had fibbed and I wasn't all that clever, or all that special? What if I was bright but would never dazzle? What if . . . Then I felt the cold and bitter slap of loneliness.

I fell backwards onto the bed and stared at the cracks on the off-white ceiling. Did they reflect the lines of destiny on my palm? Had I chosen the right path out of plainness? There had been other possibilities. Perhaps I was supposed to remain dowdy and ordinary, and happy to be so? Perhaps more learning was not the answer? Perhaps I had made the wrong choice? Had I made a fundamental mistake? Had I chosen as badly as Pandora? If I chose to open my suitcase now, would black worries whoosh out in a jingling, jangling laughing typhoon of darkness? My head ached.

I grabbed my case and rummaged desperately for that aspirin bottle. I hoped it was still in there. Yes! I opened the lid and inhaled deep breaths of Strathness until my nostrils and airways bulged with the aroma of rose, whin, honeysuckle, hawthorn blossom, wet grass and damp earth. I generously dabbed on fond memories of the Lodge, animals, pets, raucous birdsong, frail sunshine, rippling burn, storm-nipping sea breezes, fires, light, laughter and family.

I sprayed the rest of Strathness warmly around me until I was covered from head to toe in a fine green mist of childhood. I stood under it and allowed it to dry on me like a thin outer skin, which then hardened and would never wash off, and would

protect me from life's greyness and compromise and black worry. I hoped I would never outgrow it, that I would be stained indelibly with a tinge of greenness and that I would always remain proud to be slightly green.